They Sleep
Beneath the Mockingbird

They Sleep Beneath the Mockingbird

Mississippi Burial Sites and Biographies of Confederate Generals

by

Harold A. Cross

Journal of Confederate History Series

John McGlone, Editor

VOL. XII

Library of Congress Cataloging-in-Publication Data

Cross, Harold A.
They Sleep Beneath the Mockingbird
Includes bibliographical references

They Sleep Beneath the Mockingbird

DEDICATION

This book is dedicated to the memory of Private John Demit Cross, Jr., 32nd Mississippi Infantry, and Private Albert Gee Cross, 23rd Mississippi Infantry, twin sons of J. D. and Polly Cross who answered the call for volunteers in early 1861, near Ruckersville, Mississippi, and remained forever absent from their home.

ABOUT THE AUTHOR

Harold Cross is a native of Falkner, Mississippi, a small town in Tippah County. He is a graduate of Mississippi State University and earned his Masters Degree from Mississippi College. An adjunct lecturer of military history, Cross has taught numerous community college and university courses.

A veteran Air Force Pilot and current member of the Mississippi National Guard, his military decorations include the Legion of Merit, Meritorious Service Medal, and Aerial Achievement Medal. He is a command pilot with over 5,000 flying hours including combat time in Operation Desert Storm (Persian Gulf) and Operation Just Cause (Panama), and was an "outstanding graduate" of the National Defense University, Washington, D. C.

Harold Cross served as Executive Director of the Mississippi Workers' Compensation Commission and Assistant Director of the Department of Economic Development. He is now President of Cross Administrative Services, Inc,. a consulting firm for workers' compensation assigned risk and self insurance.

His wife, Carolyn, is a teacher of the gifted and they have two sons, Daniel and John.

They sleep beneath the mockingbird
Magnolia and the pine,
Fragrant dogwood forests
And honeysuckle vine.

'Neath fresh green fields of clover
Where deer and rabbit play,
Warm and sandy wetlands
Along the coastal bay.

By the famous rolling river
The scenic red clay hills
The black soil of the prairie
And Delta cotton fields.

In dear ole Mississippi
Beside the men they led
They rest in peaceful solitude
With shrines above their head.

Generals of the warriors
Who proudly wore the gray
And fought for things so dearly loved,
So cherished in their day.

Oh, sleep ye dear commander
No threat can now be heard
Beneath the sweet Magnolia
And gentle Mockingbird.

H. A. Cross

FOREWORD

When I began research on this book I was just vaguely familiar with a few of the names of the thirty three generals of the Confederate army whose remains lie gently embraced by Mississippi's soil. Their names that once glowed brilliantly throughout the South have long since faded into the shadows of generals such as Robert E. Lee, "Stonewall" Jackson, and Nathan Bedford Forrest - faded so deeply that with only rare exceptions they are erased from the memories of the current generation of Mississippians and in some instances their markers have disappeared from our cemeteries. But their remains are still with us, in Jackson, Corinth, Okolona, Aberdeen, Biloxi, Vicksburg, Natchez, "Doro" Plantation, Magnolia, Port Gibson, Greensboro, Blue Mountain, Holly Springs, Oxford, Columbus, "Arcole" Plantation, and Brandon.

My research introduced me to these giants among our forefathers and I got to know them very well. I was amazed at their virtues of self discipline, leadership, resourcefulness, and uncompromising dedication to their cause. By 1861, these men were very influential in their communities, had gained education, political notoriety, economic comforts, and in many cases substantial military fame from the Mexican War of 1846, yet they quickly answered the call to take up arms to defend their cause not unlike the minutemen and patriots of the American Revolution, knowing full well that it may cost them all their worldly possessions, their influence, and possibly even their lives.

They were present in almost all major conflicts of the Civil War, gallantly leading such Mississippi units as the University Grays, Rankin Grays, Tippah Rebels, Tallahatchie Rifles, and Raymond Fencibles through the long and bitter fight. In most instances the war did cost them their economic possessions, their professional positions, limbs, and in some cases their lives, but they did not shrink nor waver from their duty, even in times of indescribable hardship and apparent hopelessness and, to a man, the ones who survived the great conflict exercised the same vigor and energy toward the re-unification of the nation and service to their state. They were a close fraternity of very brave and virtuous men who commanded the highest degree of respect from their fellow warriors both North and South throughout their lives.

Some lived to age gracefully, regain their wealth and influence, and die quietly in their homes with their families near, a few met violent death in the war. Three were assassinated, one was killed in a street gunfight, three became Governor, two were college presidents, one a United States Senator, and others held judgeships and other high level offices. Masses gathered around them at reunions just to touch them or shake their aging hands. Thousands turned out for their funerals and many parents lifted their small children up to their biers to look at their noble repose in death. Grown men wept openly at their grave sites as they were lowered into the ground.

I have visited each grave site and as I stood there silently contemplating their daring experiences, I recalled the phrase etched on the Mississippi War Memorial; "Time will not dim the glory of their deeds". It is my sincere hope that this publication will in some small way serve to perpetuate the memory of their lives as well as the many thousands of Mississippians and others who followed them into battle. I trust that it will serve as a continual awareness of the final resting places in Mississippi of these thirty three generals of the Confederacy who so indelibly carved their names on the pages of our history. They belong not in the shadows but fully abreast in the front ranks with Lee, Jackson, and Forrest.

It was my objective to include only the generals of the regular Confederate Army who are interred in the State of Mississippi, exclusive of the State Militia or breveted officers. In addition to a few original poems by the author, I have revived some of the poetry originally published in issues of *The Confederate Veteran,* a monthly magazine which was most surely read by the surviving generals themselves. Every attempt has been made at accuracy of detail.

In cases where the sources presented differing facts, the preponderance of evidence was followed.

TABLE OF CONTENTS

GREENWOOD CEMETERY
JACKSON

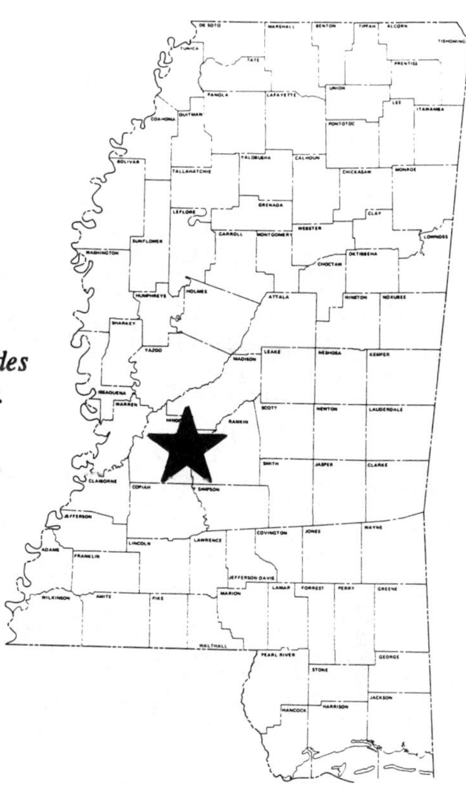

Brig. Gen. Daniel Weisiger Adams
Brig. Gen. William Wirt Adams
Brig. Gen. William Barksdale
Brig. Gen. Samuel Wragg Ferguson
Brig. Gen. Richard Griffith
Brig. Gen. James Argyle Smith

If we thought no more of the soldiers
Who fought for their cherished beliefs
And we marched no more in memorial parades
Nor honored their graves with our wreaths.

If we never pondered their toil and strife,
Loneliness, hunger and fears
On a hundred distant battlefields
Through many laborious years.

Nor ever considered their battle cries
Or tears their families shed,
And no longer stood in silent respect
Close by the graves of our dead.

Then we would silently loose ourselves
Our spirits depleted and hollow,
With the things we hold so important today
Extinguished by those who will follow.

H. A. Cross

Greenwood Cemetery is located one block northwest of the Mississippi State Capitol Building on North West Street.

Brig. Gen. Daniel Weisiger Adams, C. S. A.
1821-1872

The crude ambulance wagon dashed wildly from the raging Shiloh battlefield enroute to Corinth loaded with wounded Confederate soldiers. It was a very rough ride. The narrow road was muddy from the spring rains and almost impassable as artillery pieces and reinforcements rushed in the opposite direction toward the terrible battle. Among the most critically wounded inside the ambulance wagon was Col. Daniel Adams who had been shot in the temple just behind the right eye as he gallantly led his Mississippians in a successful charge into the peach orchard against Union General Benjamin Prentiss' division. He had long since lost consciousness and appeared to the attendants to have stopped breathing, so, thinking him dead, they threw him over the side into the mud to lighten the overloaded wagon. A few hours later as elements of the 10th Mississippi regiment were falling back from Shiloh toward Corinth on the same road, they saw they muddy body of Daniel Adams moving and discovered that he was indeed alive. They brought him to Corinth where after many months of care he recovered, permanently losing sight in his right eye but rejoining his regiment to fight again.

Daniel Adams later saw action at Perryville, Kentucky and Vicksburg, Mississippi. He was again wounded both at Murfreesboro and Chickamauga where he also taken prisoner. After his exchange he was promoted to brigadier general, given command of a brigade of cavalry, placed in charge of the district of Central Alabama and later the entire State of Alabama north of the coast region. He was singled out many times by his superiors for conspicuous gallantry and "extraordinary judgment and courage and unparalleled cheerfulness under suffering."It was said of General Daniel Adams that his intrepidity and skill proved that he was born to be a soldier. He was called "the bravest of the brave." Nothing he did before or since the war gave him as much challenge as the command of his military units, and he only regretted that he was not given command of larger forces.

When the war ended he visited Europe and resided briefly in New York but eventually settled in New Orleans becoming a very prominent attorney of that city and maintaining an active role in public affairs. It was there that Daniel Adams fought his final battle on June 13, 1872.

A sweltering heat wave had hit New Orleans in the middle of June. General Daniel Adams and his law partner, former Governor (and Brigadier General) P. O. Hebert, after calling on various clients were relieved to finally get back to their law office and out of the stifling heat. It was 3:30 p.m., the hottest part of the Thursday afternoon, as Mr. T. W. Boland, a third law partner, cordially welcomed his two law associates upon their return. The three men sat down, began discussing politics, then shifted their conversation to one of their current cases. General Adams analysis of the case so impressed Mr. Boland that he suggested that the General write it in a brief. General Adams moved over to his desk and began to write. After a few sentences the general suddenly stopped writing. His glasses fell from his face and the head which had been so brutally wounded at Shiloh slowly crumpled down on the desk beside the unfinished brief and a book entitled Phillips Practice. The brave spirit that so boldly led his troops through years of hard fighting in the great Civil War was slowly yielding. His work was finished. Mr. Boland and Governor Hebert quickly rushed to his assistance. General Adams mumbled something about terrible pain in the back of his head. His last words were "send for the doctor, I feel very badly." Medical aid was summonsed from Dr. White and Dr. Brickell. A few hours later, Gen. Daniel Adams silently slipped away onto "fame's eternal camping ground."

Dr. Brickell gave a death certificate stating that death was caused from sunstroke. Other physicians believed that it was the indirect result of the severe head wound from Shiloh exacerbated by the great mental strain of his practice and exposure to the extremely hot weather. General Adam's body was taken to his residence at 212 St. Charles Street, between Julia and St. Joseph streets for visitation by his many friends in New Orleans. His strongest attachments were always to Jackson Mississippi, the scene of his early years, the home of his brother Wirt, and where his father, Judge Adams had been president of the Union Bank, so it was chosen as his final resting place. The following day the body was brought by train to Jackson, accompanied by his brother Wirt, and arriving amidst an immense concourse of friends many of whom served with him in battle. The pall bearers that accompanied the body were Gen. P. G. T. Beauregard, Gen. P. O. Hebert, Harry T. Hays, Jeff Thompson, Col. Dolhonde, J. H. Wingfield, D. A. Wilson, Emanuel Blessey and T. L. Maxwell. He was laid to rest in Greenwood Cemetery in the family plot.

Daniel Weisiger Adams was born in Kentucky and moved with his family to Natchez as a very young child. His father was U. S. District Judge George Adams. Young Daniel was educated in law at the University of Virginia and returned to Mississippi subsequently to become a State Senator from Hinds County the first year he was old enough to hold that office under the Constitution. His father had been maliciously defamed by Vicksburg newspaper editor James Hagan in 1843. Daniel, in defense of his father's integrity had an altercation which resulted in his killing Mr. Hagan under circumstances which strongly suggested self defense. Daniel Adams was tried for murder in Hinds County and acquitted.

His obituary in the Jackson newspaper reflected the strong affection for General Daniel Adams:

"We cannot attempt to sketch the incidents and details of his life. The labor would be superfluous. His countrymen to whose cause he devoted his greatest efforts, knew him well. He was brave, manly, warm-hearted and generous. He possessed high qualities of head and heart which entitled him to prominence among his fellows wherever he moved. He was the personification of knightly courage. To his enemy he was unyielding; to his friend his affections were prodigal. The gallant soldier and devoted patriot will not soon be forgotten."

The New Orleans Daily Picayune of June 14, 1872 quoted a Mississippi officer who knew General Adams well in the field as follows:

"As a soldier, no braver man ever mingled in the turmoil, the dangers and the flame of battle. He was there the "beau ideal" of intrepid chivalry. Whilst thus lion-hearted in the fiercest conflict, he was as tender as a woman to the sufferings of his comrades in arms."

A marker in memory of Gen. Daniel Adams is located in the Confederate portion of Greenwood Cemetery. His actual grave site is west of that location, unmarked, next to his brother, Gen. Wirt Adams.

Brig. Gen. William Wirt Adams, C. S. A.
1819-1888

It was 2:15 in Jackson, Mississippi, on a beautiful spring Tuesday afternoon, May 1, 1888. Jacksonians busily shuffled along the side-walks as carriages and horseback riders moved gracefully along the streets. Two men were approaching each other from opposite directions on President Street near the corner of Amite. The gentleman walking northbound was one of Mississippi's most admired citizens, Gen. Wirt Adams, a former planter, banker, two term legislator, fearless Texas Indian fighter of the 1830's, ubiquitous cavalry officer in the Civil War, and Jackson postmaster. He had just left the post office and was walking with his friend Ned Farrish. Approaching southbound on President street was twenty-five year old John H. Martin, the aggressive editor of "The New Mississippian" an emerging Jackson newspaper of that time. Mr. Martin had recently published three offensive articles which indicted the character, honor and propriety of General Adams.

As the two men approached close enough to recognize each other, General Adams shouted "You damn rascal, I have stood enough from you!" Mr. Farish, who was walking alongside the general recalled John Martin replying "If you don't like it...." as he reached in his pocket and drew his Colt 41 six shooter. General Adams quickly produced his Colt 44 six shooter and both men began firing almost simultaneously. The normal businesslike atmosphere of downtown Jackson was suddenly jolted by the sharp sound of gunfire and bystanders in panic scurried for cover. Martin quickly ducked behind a large china tree on the outer edge of the pavement and continued to fire as General Adams ran up to the tree and around it to fire into Mr. Martin. Both men were fatally wounded and died in less than a minute from the time the first shot was fired. Martin received wounds to his leg and the right side of his chest. He whispered "I am dead" and breathed no more. General Adams was hit directly in the heart by Martin's fourth shot and died instantly.

When spectators emerged from their frantic search for cover at the corner of President and Amite streets, a gallant General who had fought bravely on the deadly fields of Shiloh, operated his cavalry in vulnerable positions around the Union flanks at Vicksburg, waged a running battle with Gen. William Tecumseh Sherman to limit his destruction in Mississippi to the Meridian area, denied Grierson access to Natchez, and fought in the last engagement of regular troops in the war near Northpoint, Alabama under Gen. Nathan Bedford Forrest's command, lay dead from his wound inflicted by a young newspaper editor. Gen. William Wirt Adams was interred in Greenwood Cemetery and lies at rest beside the unmarked grave of his brother, Brig. Gen. Daniel Adams who died sixteen years earlier.

Wirt Adams, the son of Judge George Adams had moved with his family to Natchez from his birthplace in Kentucky when he was only six years old. After obtaining a strong education he enlisted to fight in the Texas Indian Wars of 1830, and helped defeat the great Cherokee chief "Old Bowles" on the Neches River along with Albert Sidney Johnston, the Texas Secretary of War. He later gained substantial wealth in the banking business in Jackson and Vicksburg and exercised his influence as a two term State Legislator from 1851 to 1859, framing the first general laws on levee protection.

By the time of the outbreak of hostilities in 1861, Wirt Adams had obtained wealth, notoriety, political success and was offered the position of Postmaster General of the Confederate States. However, he opted to go to the field to command a cavalry unit, the First Mississippi Cavalry. This unit provided rear guard protection to Adams old friend Albert Sydney Johnston during General Johnston's retreat from Bowling Green to Nashville after the fall of Fort Donelson, and were first in the battle at Shiloh. Wirt Adams and his first cavalry aided General Forrest's cavalry in their stunning rear guard action after the battle of Shiloh which denied the Union pursuit of General Breckinridge's forces. Adam's First Cavalry saw action at Corinth with Gen. Earl Van Dorn and at Iuka, Booneville, and Burnsville, they continued to harass federal movements.

His presence was strongly felt in Washington County as he guarded plantations, scouted Union movements along the river near Vicksburg, and was the eyes and ears of General Pemberton as to General Sherman's movements. While at Warrenton, Grand Gulf, Port Gibson, and Natchez, General Adams constantly pursued and severely limited Union General Grierson's forces during their aggressive raid into Mississippi. General Adams played a major part in the battle of Raymond, covered Gregg's retreat and was constantly in action throughout the Champion Hill engagement. He was given command of cavalry in the department of Western Mississippi and Eastern Louisiana, destroyed the Union ironclad "Patrol" on the Yazoo River and later joined with Nathan Bedford Forrest to meet Croxton's Brigade at Tuscaloosa, Alabama.

In 1880 Wirt Adams was appointed State revenue agent and later Jackson postmaster by President Cleveland. Ironically, after peace had been realized, after Mississippi's economy was finally recovering, and in the middle of a normal business day, the fatal engagement came for Gen. Wirt Adams—not in a dashing cavalry charge, amidst the confusion of the battlefield with its portentous sounds of wounded men, whining of terrified horses, deafening cannonade and withering musket fire—but from the end of a pistol hastily fired in a temperamental altercation that could have so easily been avoided.

Col. George Moorman eulogized his friend Wirt Adams with the closeness only war veterans could truly understand:

"......he possessed every attribute of patriotism, nobleness, goodness and gentleness necessary to have distinguished him in any age or in any land.

In the movements of the army, I reached Mississippi at an impressible age. Our headquarters were in the Governor's Mansion at Jackson, Mississippi, and I can well remember him there as the companion and intimate friend of William Yerger, William L. Sharkey, A. H. Handy, Walker Brooke, George L. Potter, Albert G. Brown and Amos R. Johnston, a race of intellectual giants, alas! all gone, but constituting a glittering galaxy which is fixed forever in the firmament of Mississippi's glory. Two others not mentioned of that grand coterie of his bosom friends yet linger and join with us in lamentations for our glorious dead, one of whom is the transcendent genius, their peerless chieftain and beloved sage of Beauvoir, the other, the gifted intellect, the true citizen, and matchless friend, Ethelebert Barksdale.

Friend, patriot, hero, farewell; while life lasts your name will be enshrined in our hearts, and will ever awaken chords of glorious music upon the harp of memory.

He has not died. There is no grave for glory.
No shroud, no coffin, no imprisoning clay
All that was mortal of him lies in ashes.
All that was best of him is yours today."

Imposing monument erected at the grave site of Gen. Wirt Adams in Greenwood Cemetery. His brother, Daniel, lies adjacent to the south in an unmarked grave.

Brig. Gen. William Barksdale, C. S. A.
1821-1863

The largest battle ever recorded in the Western Hemisphere was raging into its second day near the little town of Gettysburg, Pennsylvania, on July 2, 1863. It was a battle destined to result in more American casualties than ten years of fighting in Vietnam, and conclude with a Union victory .

General William Barksdale's brigade of Mississippians, the thirteenth, seventeenth, eighteenth, and twenty first regiments, representing the finest troops the Army of Northern Virginia had to offer, were preparing to advance into the engagement. The battle hardened, highly disciplined, well accoutered troops of McLaws' division, Longstreet's Corps, were deeply fond of their flamboyant commander, Brig. Gen. William Barksdale. He had represented his State proudly in Congress, was an outstanding attorney, loving father and husband, and upon the death of Brig. Gen. Richard Griffith at Savage Station in 1862, had assumed command of the Mississippi brigade, leading them daringly at Antietam, Fredericksburg, and Chancellorsville. As General Barksdale marshaled his troops with the enemy clearly in sight he got the nod from McLaws and shouted to his fourteen hundred men, "Attention, Mississippians!, Battalions Forward!" The brigade raised the rebel yell and surged forward with General Barksdale riding at least 50 yards ahead wearing a bright red sash around his waist and waving his sword over his head. They were the "Kemper Legion," "New Albany Greys," "Vicksburg Southrons," "Hurricane Rifles," "Panola Vindicators," "Madison Guards," "Mississippi College Rifles," "Jackson Revengers," "Camden Rifles," "Magnolia Guards," and many other companies of proud Mississippians following their fearless leader into battle. General James Longstreet, his corps commander, later wrote;

"it was the grandest charge that was ever seen by mortal man, ... I saw him as far as the eye could follow, still ahead of his men leading them on."

On through the Peach Orchard, across Emmitsburg road and into the bushes and trees of Plum Run, toward their objective of Little Round Top, fighting fiercely and absorbing continuous fusillades of fire from very close range musketry and artillery in the searing heat of the July sun. Barksdale's Mississippians were gaining the field against a Union force almost four times their size. Union General Joseph Carr, observing the effectiveness of General Barksdale's fearless leadership and conspicuous presence on the battlefield, ordered the Eleventh New Jersey regiment to "bring down the officer on the white horse!" An entire company focused its fire in the direction of Barksdale. A rifle ball tore through his left leg just above the knee breaking the bone but through the excruciating pain he led on. Very shortly thereafter a cannon ball almost completely tore off his left foot, and although becoming weak from the loss of blood, he continued to lead the ferocious brigade of Mississippians into one of the most violent engagements of the Civil War. Suddenly a large piece of grapeshot cut savagely through his chest knocking him from his horse where, in the frantic confusion, he was left on the field with the dead and dying.

As night fell on the bloody battlefield the pitiful mourns of the wounded could be heard all across the fields pleading for water and help. Barksdale's brigade alone had suffered over 700 casualties. A Confederate prisoner reported to his Union captors that General Barksdale lay wounded or dead upon the field and the Union officer dispatched Pvt. David Parker and two other soldiers to find the general. Later, after the war, Pvt. Parker conveyed to General Barksdale's brother Ethelbert, by letter, the events of the night:

"We searched among the dead and wounded until about 11 at night when we found him. He was suffering from bleeding inwardly and suffering very much. I immediately sat on the ground, took his head in my lap and gave him coffee that I had in my canteen from a spoon, as he could swallow but a small amount at a time. His mind was clear. He stated who he was and first told us that we could not carry him into our lines without a stretcher and (needed) more help as he weighed 240 pounds. Two men went for help. He commenced by telling me that he was dying; that he was leaving a good and loving wife and two sons, if I remember right - 11 and 13. Now I will use his words as near as I can remember, 'Oh my wife, It will be hard for her. Tell her that my last words were words of love to her. But my boys! Oh, it seems that I cannot leave them. Their loss they will not fully comprehend. They need a father. Many times have I thought and planned for their future, and, oh, I loved them, so to leave them is the hardest struggle I ever knew. But tell them all that I died like a brave man, that I led my men fearlessly in the fight. ....and tell them all, all my friends, wife and children. I do not regret giving my life in a cause that I believe to be right, but one thing I do regret is that I could not have lived to have done more for the cause. Oh, that I might again lead my men, but tell them that I die content that my last day's work was well done. I feel that I am most gone. May God ever watch over and take care of my dear wife and , oh, my boys, may God be a father to them. Tell them to be good men and brave, always defend the right.' He became unconscious talking of his family. We carried him on the hill to the left of Cemetery Hill. He breathed his last about daylight or a little before."

Upon being brought into the Union lines on a stretcher, General Barksdale was attended by Alfred Thorley Hamilton, Assistant surgeon, 148th Pennsylvania regiment who described him: ".. he was large, corpulent, refined in appearance, bald, and his general physical and mental make up indicated firmness, endurance, vigor, quick perception and ability to succeed whether politician, civilian, or warrior. He told me that he was a member of Congress under Pierce and Buchanan. He asked about our strength and was answered that heavy reinforcements are coming. He said that Lee would show us a trick before morning, that before we knew it Ewell would be thundering in our rear."

Surgeon Hamilton prescribed morphine and assured him that his wounds were mortal. He died in the early morning hours of July 3, and was initially buried in the yard of the Jacob Hummelbaugh farmhouse just a few feet from where he died. Later, at the request of the Barksdale family, his body was disinterred and brought to Washington, D.C. for embalming and to await shipment to Mississippi.

In January, 1867, the body was finally brought back to Jackson, Mississippi, by Lieutenant Harris Barksdale, the nephew of the general who had served with him at Gettysburg. A committee of Jacksonians met the train bearing the gallant warrior at the depot at one o'clock on the afternoon of January 9, 1867, and transported it to the old capitol where it lay in state for thousands to pass by and pay their last respects. After the funeral later that afternoon the members of his Masonic Lodge escorted the body of General Barksdale to Greenwood Cemetery in Jackson for burial in the Barksdale family plot. Colonel Walter of Jackson officiated at the graveside as "Master of Masonic Ceremonies", and delivered the following remarks to the mourners standing at the open grave site in Greenwood Cemetery:

"We are before the grave of no ordinary citizen. In all the relations of life, General Barksdale challenged the esteem and compelled the respect of his fellow man. As a friend he was true and trusty; as a son, dutiful and obedient; as a husband, tender and loving; and as a father, affectionate yet controlling. As a citizen, his manly frankness and sterling virtues won him friends; as a lawyer, his genial nature and commanding talents secured audiences; and as a statesman, his nervous eloquence, his sound counsels and incorruptible integrity reflected honor upon himself and his constituents. When the hour of peril came to the South, he sought the post of danger, and the halo of heroism illumined the chaplet of the statesman. At the head of his noble Mississippians, he led the van on the ensanguined field, and wherever blows fell fastest and freest, his manly form was seen and his clarion voice was heard. In the frightful carnival of death at Gettysburg, he yielded to that conqueror whose command is law and his gallant spirit went home. And now,

'The trumpet may sound, the loud cannons rattle,
He heeds not, he hears not, he's free from all pain,
He sleeps his last sleep, he has fought his last battle,
No sound can awake him to glory again.'

His form lies lifeless before us. His eye that sparkled at the tale of mirth or moistened at the pleading of suffering, is now closed, and his hand that was ever open to charity, is now in the history of a long, useful and brilliant career. It bids us imitate his virtues, emulate his courage, and copy his acts of goodness and worth, so that when the final message comes to us, loving friends will stand at our bier, drop the sympathetic tear in our grave, and cherish with sacred sorrow, our memory."

The former Congressman, lawyer, statesman, and gallant military leader who served in the Mexican war with the Mississippi volunteers and with distinction at Manassas, Edward's Ferry, Richmond, Antietam Fredericksburg, Chancellorsville and Gettysburg had come home at last. His wife, Narcissa, whom he remembered so lovingly in his dying moments on the Gettysburg battlefield, died on March 23rd, 1875, at 3 o'clock p.m., at the residence of her son Ethelbert C. Barksdale at his Holly Bend plantation in Yazoo County and was taken to Jackson for interment beside her beloved husband. She was eulogized by the Jackson Weekly Clarion as follows;

"General Barksdale was justly proud of his wife, proud of her intellect, proud of her gentleness and grace, and, above all, proud of her devotion to himself. Her life had been a very happy one until the battle of Gettysburg; but when her gallant husband yielded up his noble spirit on that blood stained field, the world had no further charms for her. The earth grew silent when his voice departed, and she dropped like a bird with a broken wing. There was no rebound under that terrible blow, and though she went through life without complaining, it was apparent that her heart was not with the things of this world, and that it was yearning to be at rest by the side of him who was so long the pride and joy of her life. The rest for which she sighed has come at last. The weary heart is at peace."

Confederate marker in memory of General Barksdale located in the Confederate section of Jackson's Greenwood Cemetery. His actual grave site is about one hundred yards to the west of this spot in the Barksdale family plot just west of his nephew, Harris Barksdale, and is unmarked.

Brig. Gen. Samuel Wragg Ferguson, C. S. A.
1834-1917

The firing at Fort Sumter had just ceased, Union Maj. Robert Anderson indicated that he was ready to surrender his 68 man garrison and Confederate Gen. Pierre Gustave Toutant Beauregard sent his aide-de-camp, Lt. Samuel Wragg Ferguson to accept the surrender. After receiving the keys to the stockade from Major Anderson, Ferguson turned and personally lowered the federal colors hoisting upon the ramparts of Fort Sumter the first banner of the Confederacy to fly over a Union fort, the Palmetto flag of his native State of South Carolina. This was one of his proudest moments.

Samuel Wragg Ferguson was descended from a family deeply rooted in military history. His father had served as an officer in the War of 1812, and his grandfather was a member of the council of safety which refused to surrender Charleston in the Revolutionary War and was arrested by the British and banished. In 1852, Samuel entered West Point and graduated in the class of 1857. As a lieutenant he was with Albert Sydney Johnston in the First United States Dragoons and took part in quelling the Mormon uprising as his first assignment. Later he was in charge of escorting wagon trains westward, and was in Walla Walla, Washington when he learned of South Carolina's secession from the Union, whereupon he immediately resigned his commission and offered his services to the Confederate army.

After Fort Sumter, Samuel Wragg Ferguson participated in the first Battle of Manassas, then Shiloh. He was appointed lieutenant colonel of the 28th regiment of Mississippi Cavalry which included such proud units as the "Buckner Light Horses" "Mayson Dragoons," "Panola Cavalry," and "McAfee Hussars." They scouted for Union activity around Vicksburg and the Mississippi River protecting plantations and vital waterways. He was married in 1862 to Kate Lee of Washington County who was an excellent horse rider. Kate accompanied the general in all of his campaigns afterwards and took very copious notes on camp life. In the summer of 1863 General Ferguson was made brigadier general of cavalry, operated in Mississippi, Tennessee, Alabama, and Georgia and was almost constantly on skirmish around General Sherman's army.

General Ferguson was described as a most efficient military leader, cool and courageous, although his promotion to major general was protested by Gen. Joe Wheeler. The tenacious General Ferguson was said to have been the last Confederate soldier to leave Atlanta prior to its fall to General Sherman. Following the surrender of General Lee at Appomattox General Ferguson and his cavalry escorted President Jefferson Davis from Charlotte to Abbeville and was with President Davis at his last Council of War.

He was with Mississippians during most of his service in the war and he came to Greenville, Mississippi, to settle afterwards. He studied law, was admitted to the bar in 1866, and in 1885 he was appointed to the Mississippi River Commission by President Arthur. Ferguson previously served as President of the Board of the Mississippi Levee Commission. Lake Ferguson in Greenville was named in his honor. However, his fortunes later took a bad turn in Greenville as he was the target of several lawsuits concerning real estate transactions around the city. He relocated to Biloxi and later became ill. At the age of 82 he entered the State Hospital in Jackson, where he died with his family in attendance on February 3, 1917. The noble veteran who served so bravely in our Nation's costliest war had lived long enough to see the opening of World War I, the "war to end all wars."

General Ferguson's remains were carried to the H.M. Taylor undertaking parlor in Jackson for open visitation. On February 4, funeral services were conducted by the Reverend William Green and he was buried in the Confederate section of Jackson's Greenwood Cemetery along with the many hundreds of other fallen soldiers of the Confederacy. The active pall bearers for General Ferguson were; George B. Power, William Yerger, A. C. Walthall, J. R. McDowell, C. H. Manship, R. H. Green, T. P. Barr, Henry Yerger, and Joe Robinson.

His obituary stated that; "... his death marked the passing of a splendid figure, another of the gray clad heroes of the sixties has gone to the silent bivouac of the dead, to the sorrow of his loved ones and his friends."

General Ferguson's grave stone is located in the Confederate section of Jackson's Greenwood Cemetery near his actual unmarked grave.

Brig. Gen. Richard Griffith, C. S. A.
1814-1862

He was a Pennsylvania school teacher and an honor graduate of Ohio University before moving to Vicksburg to teach in a private school. Richard Griffith was described as "a fine physique, tall and well proportional, dark brown hair inclined to curl, blue eyes, regular features and fair but ruddy complexion with graceful though military carriage, his was a combination and form indeed where every god did seem to set his seal to give the assurance of man, a devoted husband and father, a loyal and true friend, broad in charity."

Offering his services at the outbreak of the Mexican War in 1846, he was recruited by Lt. Col. Jefferson Davis into his famous regiment, the 1st Mississippi Rifles and made adjutant of that regiment, holding the rank of first lieutenant. Davis and Griffith became very close friends as the Mississippi Rifles distinguished themselves at the Battle of Buena Vista and after the war their friendship continued to grow as Griffith settled in Jackson becoming a prominent banker and businessman.

They both had remarkably successful careers in politics before the war, Davis becoming a United States Senator, Griffith a two term State Treasurer, and later

United States Marshal of Mississippi's Southern district. Richard Griffith was present as Mississippi's ordinance of secession was passed and although Jefferson Davis offered his close friend a position of high esteem in the Confederate Government he respectfully declined opting instead to utilize his military talents in the field.

Even before the firing on Fort Sumter Griffith recruited the "Raymond Fencibles," armed them with newly improved Springfields, and made them a showcase of discipline and order. By early May, 1861, Griffith and his "Raymond Fencibles" were on there way to Corinth, the great rallying point of many units organizing for further service. As they departed from the train station at Bolton, the parting scene was mixed with sorrow and joy. "The cries of mothers, sisters, sweethearts, and friends were drowned by the boom of cannon and the notes of fife and drum." At Corinth they were united with the "Vicksburg Sharpshooters," the "Sardis Blues," the "Lawrence Rifles," the "Pettus Relief," the "Charlie Clark Rifles," the "Claiborne Guards," and the "Satartia Rifles," to constitute the 12th Mississippi Infantry, with Richard Griffith as their colonel.

The 12th Mississippi was assigned to the Confederate Army in Virginia and by November, 1861, Griffith had been promoted to brigadier general and given command of four other Mississippi regiments, the 13th, 17th, 18th, and 21st, forming the 3rd Mississippi Infantry Brigade, assigned to Macgruder's Division.

It was during the Battle of Seven Days around Richmond on 29 June, 1862 that General Griffith's brigade, having been held in reserve, were ordered into action against the enemy's rear guard. As Griffith's brigade was taking a more forward position for attack the Union artillery asserted their location and opened up a brisk barrage of artillery fire near the railroad at Savage Station and into the middle of the Griffith's brigade. It was at this point in time that half an exploded rifled artillery shell tore into the left groin of General Griffith, missing everyone else. According to an eyewitness;

"a wicket shell struck the railroad section house just in our front, and exploded, a piece of which we distinctly saw pass over our heads. In falling it struck General Griffith on the thigh, tearing the flesh down to his knee, while he was sitting on his horse near the fort just in our rear."

Troops who were jubilant just a few moments earlier at the prospect of ensuing battle were stunned to see their commander grimace and fall from his horse into the arms of Colonel Inge of Corinth with a gaping wound profusely bleeding and in agonizing pain. Many of his beloved troops gathered around and assisted him to the rear. Asking if the wound was fatal and being advised that it was, the brave general commented;

"Am I thus to die? If it is thy decree, Oh God, I murmur not, but how willingly would I have yielded up my life if I could have been spared to have led my boys and served my country through this day's struggle; but they will do their duty."

Command was passed to Col. William Barksdale and the fight went on as General Griffith was carried to the rear. As word spread about General Griffith's injury, President Davis, who had recently been ordered to the rear of the action by General Lee for his safety came forward again to find his old friend. As he located General Griffith he knelt down and grasped his dear friend's hand and exclaimed, "My dear boy, I hope you are not seriously hurt." Rapidly losing consciousness from the loss of blood, the forty-seven year- old general replied; "I am afraid it is fatal—good-bye colonel."

President Davis remained with General Griffith and had him hastily transported to Richmond to the home of Mr. Purcell, sitting by his bedside until his death later that night. The funeral of Gen. Richard Griffith was held the next day in the Confederate White House attended by the President, his cabinet and hundreds of mourners. Gen. Robert E. Lee delivered a touching eulogy of General Griffith at the next parade inspection of his troops. The President personally notified General Griffith's wife, Sallie Ann Eliza Whitfield, of the tragic news, and as word spread of his death, concerned citizens in Jackson met to plan the return of General Griffith's body. Placed in charge of the arrangements for the transfer was a committee composed of the following: Judge William Yerger, Dr. F. T. Knapp, Hon. E. M. Yerger, Messrs. T. J. Wharton, F. T. Cooper, J. D. Freeman, J. D. Stuart, C. R. Dickson, C. H. Manship, C. S. Knapp, A. N. Kimball, and General Wharton. The body was returned and interred in Greenwood Cemetery in Jackson amidst hundreds of mourners.

Gen. Richard Griffith's obituary in the July 7, 1862 edition of the Clarion Ledger read;

"a more chivalrous spirit never winged its flight from a field of glory to realms of unfading bliss. He died as he would have wished to die with his face to the foe at the head of his gallant brigade in line of battle and in the moment of victory. In the language of the dispatch from President Davis who was his companion in arms in the war with Mexico and through life cherished for him the most fraternal affection, 'He died as he had lived, an honest man, a gallant soldier, and a devoted friend."

General Griffith's remains lie under this marker in the north-east quadrant of Jackson's Greenwood Cemetery next to his wife, Sallie, and three blocks north of the street which bears his name.

Brig. Gen. James Argyle Smith, C. S. A.
1831-1901

The early days of December, 1901, were cold and dreary. The seventy year old marshal of the Mississippi Supreme Court, former Confederate Brig. Gen. James Argyle Smith, had been overexposed to the weather and had a terrible cold. He was not able to attend the Monday afternoon sitting of the Court and went home to recuperate, but his condition began to worsen, progressing into pneumonia, the ravages of which his weakened constitution without the aid of antibiotics was unable to withstand. As his condition became critical his family gathered by his bedside at his residence on West Capitol Street. At 9 p.m. on the night of December 6, the West Point graduate who had witnessed first hand many of the decisive battles of the great Civil War, drew his last breath and according to his obituary, "joined Lee and Jackson and other Confederate leaders on the other side of the river."

He would be missed among many circles of admirers. For the last year of his life he rendered tireless service to the Mississippi Supreme Court having replaced Thomas Wharton who had retired. He was revered in the education community, serving as State Superintendent of Education for two terms beginning in 1877. President Grover Cleveland tapped him for service as an Indian Agent to North Dakota during his second term because of his noteworthy military and administrative background. But a much larger and more tightly woven fraternity would miss him most and would grieve his passing with deep piercing sorrow. They were his fellow Confederate veterans who served with him during the most difficult days of out nation's history, who laughed and cried with him, who shared the deprivations, fears and agony of sacrifice, yet still swelled with pride in each other's presence. They were a fraternity that transcended politics, religion, greed, position and even family in their camaraderie with silent awareness of each other's well being. So when "Jake" Smith's corpse was laid out for viewing in his home, the masses that filed by included many of these brethren who would pause just a little longer and appear a little sadder in their sincere payment of respect.

General Smith's funeral took place the next day at the West Side Presbyterian Church at three o'clock. The pastor, Reverend F. L. McGue, delivered an impassioned eulogy to the overflowing crowd. In addition to the members of the Supreme Court, the R. A. Smith Camp of the United Confederate Veterans attended in a body. Pall bearers John W. Clingan, R. K. Jayne, John Webb, E. H. Reber, R. H. Henry and George W. Carlisle lifted the casket to its carriage at the conclusion of the services and the mourners proceeded to Greenwood Cemetery for burial just north of hundreds of Confederate soldiers' graves.

Many thoughts of remembrance surely permeated the minds of the old veterans that day. Some would have remembered Jake Smith as a young boy growing up in Hinds and Rankin counties after moving with his parents from his birthplace in Maury County, Tennessee, and his pride in having been appointed to the United States Military Academy at West Point as a fledging young Rankin Countian in 1848, graduating in 1853. He had related to his friends the many adventures of service in the U. S. Army as a lieutenant during confrontation with the Sioux Indians in 1855, operations in "Bleeding Kansas" in '56, and the Mormon uprising in '58, then how he wrestled with the tough decision after secession, to resign his commission in lieu of drawing his sword against his adopted State of Mississippi, and his birth State of Tennessee.

James Argyle Smith was initially placed in command of an infantry company, then promoted in 1862, to major and adjutant to Gen. Leonidas Polk. By Shiloh in 1862, he was a lieutenant colonel and in command of the 2nd Tennessee Infantry, a unit which fought gallantly against the Union right wing on April 6. For his proven field command abilities he was promoted to colonel in command of the 5th Infantry Regiment of the Confederate States Army. He led them through the bloody thickets of Murfreesboro and Perryville, where he was stunningly victorious against Gen. Lovell H. Roussau's division, and on to Stone's River and the great Battle of Chickamauga where he earned promotion to brigadier general for his intrepid skills.

He was brigadier general in command of James Deshler's Texas brigade when he was intensely engaged in the savage fighting at Missionary Ridge, engaging Sherman's entire corps, checking the federal flank and protecting Bragg's vulnerable position, while receiving gunshots through both thighs. Recovering in time for the Atlanta campaign, he was again wounded but not before he and his brigade "captured three lines of the enemy's works, nineteen pieces of artillery and two standards of colors." General Smith's fearless fighters were hotly engaged at the Battle of Franklin and when Gen. Pat Cleburne was killed, Smith assumed command of his entire division for the subsequent battle of Nashville, and on into Carolina in 1865, and until the final surrender "he was equal to every emergency, suffering hardships and privations with his men, and inspiring them to heroic deeds and soldiery valor."

Yes the old veterans remembered. They remembered that at the close of the war he returned to his adopted State of Mississippi and offered his remaining energies to the betterment of society. They remembered that he came back to be with his friends, and they knew he would have wanted no higher honor than for the veterans of the R. A. Smith Camp to be standing by his grave at the moment of interment in the cemetery which embraced the remains of Barksdale, Griffith, Wirt and Daniel Adams, and hundreds of just as brave and loyal Southern soldiers.

General Smith lies under this marker next to his wife just northwest of the Confederate grave markers in Greenwood Cemetery in Jackson.

REST

WINTERGREEN CEMETERY
PORT GIBSON

Maj. Gen. Earl Van Dorn
Brig. Gen. Benjamin Grubb Humphreys

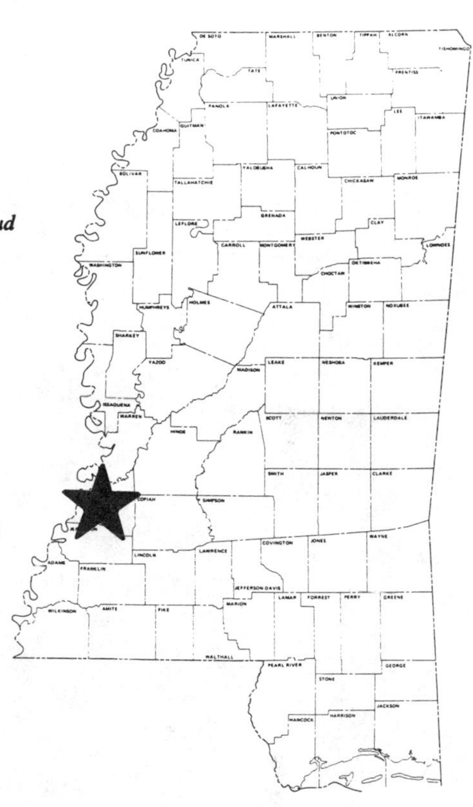

The bugles of battle! How shrilly they blew
Where the river flows under the pines,
Where the legions of gray stood heroic and true
In the smoke of the gallant old lines,
And the banners that waved where the bugles sang loud
As we watched for the rush of the foe!
They sing for me yet through the mist and the cloud
That envelopes the long, long ago.

The bugles of battle! How often they rent
The air with their nerve-piercing thrill!
How often some hero to glory they sent
In the charge for the crest of the hill!
I listen to-day for the roar in the wood,
For the crash and the sweep of the guns,
And I dream of the times when in battle once stood
For the cause of the Southland her sons.

The bugles of battle! How silent they grew
When the comrade was laid to his rest,
Above him the stars and the glistening dew
And brave folded hands on his breast,
In his jacket of gray 'neath the towering pines
By the river that slips to the sea!
We left him a gap in the gallant old lines,
From war and its wrath ever free.

The bugles of battle! They blew 'neath the arch
Of azure that bent overhead.
How often they quickened the weary one's march
As forward the long columns sped!
Sometimes in my dreams at the dusk of the day
I hear them again and again,
And the sunlight falls soft on a jacket of gray,
Where the flowers bloom fresh on the plain.

The bugles of battle! I look at my cane,
My daily companion, you see,
And back to me comes the wild fight in the lane
'Neath the far-flashing banners of Lee.
No more will they blow as they blew long ago,
The blood of a youthtime to thrill;
Forever for me and the valorous foe
The bugles of battle are still. *T.C. Harbaugh*

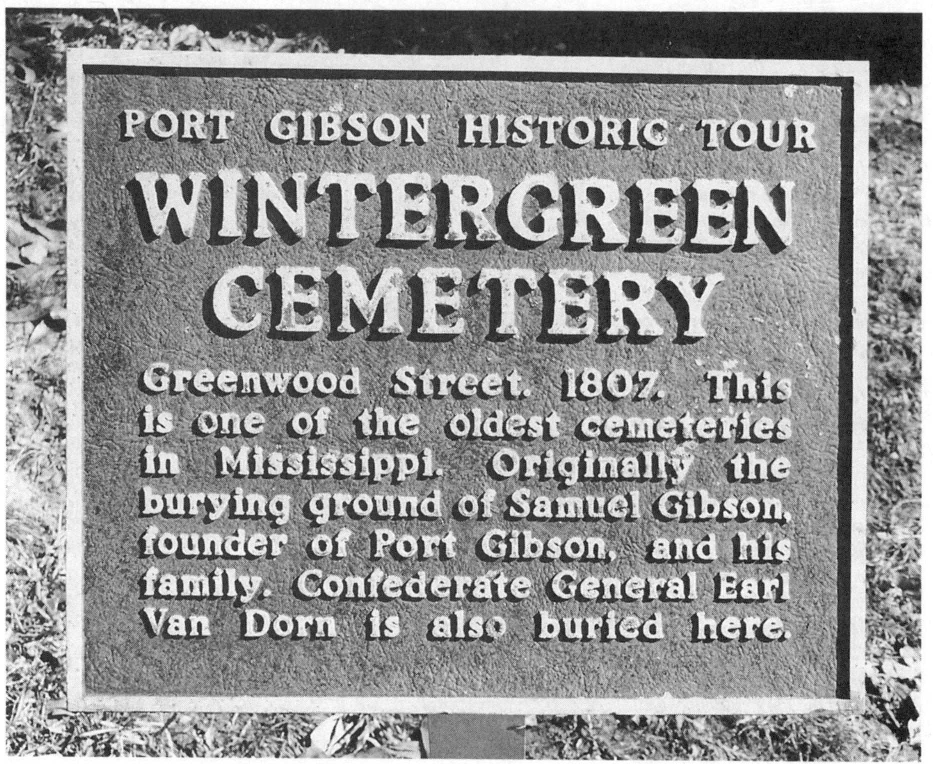

Follow highway 61 into Port Gibson, turn east on Greenwood Street.

Maj. Gen. Earl Van Dorn, C. S. A.
1820-1863

Shortly after noon on May 7, 1863, the strikingly handsome forty-three year old Maj. Gen. Earl Van Dorn sat quietly at his desk in the corner upstairs office of his headquarters building in Spring Hill, Tennessee. He had just finished a conversation with his loyal and dedicated adjutant, Maj. Manning Kimmel (father of Adm. Husband E. Kimmel of later Pearl Harbor fame.) As he conferred with other members of his staff, Dr. George Bodie Peters, a wealthy physician and landowner and husband of the vivacious young Jessie McKissack Peters arrived downstairs inquiring to see General Van Dorn. He purportedly wished to obtain a written passport that would take him safely through Confederate lines to Nashville where he claimed to have business to transact. Dr. Peters was escorted to the General's office, the two men greeted each other amiably, having been previously acquainted, the staff took their leave of the two men and went outside.

As General Van Dorn was writing out the passport at his desk, Dr. Peters produced a small caliber "parlor pistol" from his pocket and fired it directly into the back of the head of the young general from Port Gibson, Mississippi, fatally wounding him. Not hearing the report from the small caliber gun nor expecting anything amiss, the general's staff did not interfere when Dr. Peters calmly mounted his horse and rode off from the general's headquarters. About two minutes later, the young daughter of the owner of the house came vaulting out shouting that Dr. Peters had shot General Van Dorn. They found him slumped over face down in his own blood, the bullet having lodged just behind his right eye which had protruded and turned black. He lay unconscious for about four hours, then died. Dr. Peters, having stationed numerous relay horses between the crime scene and Nashville, successfully escaped.

The motive for this incident has been hotly debated for many years. There was much speculation that General Van Dorn, who was very popular with the ladies because of his knightly appearance which matched his grace and charm, had been intimately involved with Dr. Peters' beautiful wife, Jessie. She was the Doctor's third wife, and his cousin whom he had admittedly married to retain wealth in the family. Another theory that has been advanced is that Dr. Peters was on a mission of assassination for the Union for bounty as well as the protection of his own land since he had taken a Union loyalty oath in Memphis shortly before he murdered General Van Dorn and used the infidelity issue as an excuse. In any case he successfully escaped into Union hands and was never convicted of the crime, later divorcing his wife only to remarry her after the war. The charismatic and charming Jessie Peters, however, consistently denied to her death that anything improper ever occurred between her and Van Dorn.

The bullet of the assassin Peters snuffed out the life of the ideal soldier, one of daring military genius who was the epitome of Southern chivalry and bravery. This magnificent man, nicknamed "Buck" by his friends, with dark flashing blue eyes, keen intelligence, and long light chestnut colored hair had been born into an aristocratic family in Port Gibson. His father was a highly renowned Judge of revolutionary war descent and it was his great uncle, Andrew Jackson, who secured his appointment to West Point, fulfilling the ultimate dream of young Earl. He graduated in the 1842 class with Longstreet and McLaws, fought gallantly with Gen. Winfield Scott, and Col. Jefferson Davis in the Mexican War where he was cited by Generals Persifer Smith and Winfield Scott for distinguished service, bravery, and gallantry. He led fierce fighting at Chepultepec and was among the first to scale the wall. He was with General Quitman at Monterey and was wounded while entering Mexico City with General Scott.

After the Mexican War he was among an elite group of cavalry selected to rid Texas of the vicious Indian threat from the Commanche and Apache tribes. He served in this duty with Robert E. Lee, John Bell Hood, George McClellan, Albert Sydney Johnston and J.E.B. Stuart, and many other notable military leaders destined to become great generals in the Civil War. He was twice severely wounded by Indian arrows but survived to be awarded Swords of Honor upon his return home by the Mississippi Legislature and a silver service by the citizens of Port Gibson. When secession came he did not hesitate to follow his State by resigning his commission as major and commander of the first division of the Army of the Potomac.

Earl Van Dorn was first appointed brigadier general of the Mississippi Militia but soon opted to go into the Confederate Army as a colonel. He was first stationed in Texas where he captured the federal steamer "Star of the West" in Galveston Harbor. General Van Dorn's military prowess then had several setbacks. After being assigned to Virginia to organize the cavalry he returned to Arkansas to fight with General Price. His unsuccessful encounter at the Battle of Pea Ridge, Arkansas, in March, 1862, and his defeat by Rosecrans in an intense battle at Corinth which resulted in an unsuccessful attempt at court martial by Gen. John S. Bowen, was the low point of his illustrious military career along with the negative reaction of the people of Vicksburg in response to his issue of general order nine which invoked the death penalty for southerners caught trading goods with the enemy.

General Van Dorn recovered quickly, however by making a daring and highly successful raid on the federal stockpiles at Holly Springs, on December 20, 1862, capturing or destroying over three million dollars worth of federal weapons, ammunitions and food supplies along with the capture of their commander Col. Robert C. Murphey. This raid was responsible for delaying the fall of Vicksburg by at least six months. Along with Gen. Nathan Bedford Forrest's cavalry, he successfully routed Coburn's brigade at Thompson Station, Tennessee. In the latter part of April near this place he got into a heated debate with the high tempered Forrest over some accusations that were made concerning Forrest's handling of captured goods. The two generals almost engaged in a saber duel, Forrest regaining his composure after half drawing his sword and then expressing that it would be a poor example to their men for two generals to settle a dispute this way.

Then, suddenly, in the following month, one of the South's most daring cavalry officers lay dead in his headquarters, in Spring Hill, Tennessee, from a small caliber pistol fired by a cowardly noncombatant. After his body lay in state briefly at Columbia, Tennessee, for his soldiers and citizens of that area to pay their last respects, it was transported to the home of his wife in Mt. Vernon, Alabama, and in the words of an eyewitness to the funeral there:

"As we watch the immense procession of soldiers the hearse drawn by six white horses, its gorgeous array of white and black plumes, that bore the grand casket in which the dead hero lay, we thought with sorrow of the handsome face still in death and the heart-broken wife, thus cruelly widowed. His little daughter was the chief sorrower visible at his bier, the wife being too prostrated by grief to leave her room.

I have the most vivid recollection of all the incidents attending the great military procession to his grave and my journey with the Guard of Honor to Col. Godbold's house (father in law of Gen. Van Dorn) and the burial there under the sighing pines about 40 yards from the house with the exquisite Olivia weeping and clinging to my hand as she walked to the grave as the chief mourner."

General Van Dorn was buried in Mt. Vernon, Alabama, because his home of Port Gibson, Mississippi was, at the time of his murder, in enemy hands and permission could not be obtained to transport him there. Later in 1899, the sister of the distinguished soldier with the help of her son, Hon T. Marshall Miller, an ex-attorney general of Mississippi directed the remains to be disinterred and moved to the historic Wintergreen cemetery in Port Gibson to be buried by his father, Judge P. A. Van Dorn. The casket was opened after over thirty years of interment in Alabama. The remains of Major General Van Dorn were found to be in an excellent state of preservation.

"The form was clad in the Confederate gray uniform of a major-general, the belt, buckles and epaulettes being intact, and around his shoulders were the soft golden curis familiar to soldiers on a hundred battlefields as the intrepid warrior rode at the front of his men and urged them to battle."

He was re-interred in Wintergreen Cemetery facing south alongside the grave of his father and near the bodies both known and unknown of many other Confederate soldiers who lost their lives in the battle of Port Gibson. The remains of the dashing famed warrior, one of Mississippi's finest ever, are now in their eternal resting place in the shadow of huge cedars in one of the most beautiful burial grounds of our State.

General Van Dorn's remains rest next to his father, Judge P. A. Van Dorn in Port Gibson's Wintergreen Cemetery. The graves are facing South since the Judge wished to be buried facing his plantation located south of the cemetery.

Brig. Gen. Benjamin Grubb Humphreys, C. S. A.
1808-1882

Dawn was just beginning to break on the chilly Wednesday morning of December 27, 1882, as a small group of civil war veterans were gathering at the train depot in the serene and picturesque town of Port Gibson, Mississippi. Theirs was the somber task of boarding the early train to Grand Gulf to receive the body of their old friend and leader, Gen. Benjamin Grubb Humphreys, and escort it back to Port Gibson for the funeral and burial that afternoon. General Humphreys, who had yielded up his spirit on December 23 at his plantation in Itta Bena, was at last coming home to his native Claiborne County, at the end of his seventy five year life which transcended some of the most notable events of our nation's history. On the train ride to Grand Gulf many of the veterans in their solemnity no doubt pondered the life of the their fallen comrade as the wintry scenes passed by their windows.

Born on August 26, 1808, at the Hermitage Plantation on Bayou Pierre, Benjamin Humphreys was the son of the prominent planter George Humphreys and his wife Sarah, and the grandson of Ralph Humphreys who served in the Revolutionary War and had located in the "Natchez District" in 1788, during Spanish domination. As a young man Benjamin was afforded a quality education in Kentucky and New Jersey, and secured an appointment from Senator Thomas N.

Williams to West Point in 1825 with classmates Robert E. Lee, Joseph E. Johnston, Albert Sidney Johnston, and Jefferson Davis. He had everything going for him in his youth but tragedy lurked in the shadows.

First there was a Christmas party on the West Point campus in 1826 which got out of hand and turned into a near riot. Cadet Benjamin Grubb Humphreys was among the 39 cadets expelled for "breech of discipline." Then, after returning to his father's Hermitage plantation and becoming a planter, his lovely young wife, Mary McLaughlin died. To many men the despondence and rejection of those events would be overwhelming but his strong character and resolve allowed him to rise from them. He studied law and was elected to the Mississippi House of Representatives and then to the Senate as a Whig. He remarried, this time to fifteen year old Mildred Hickman Maury, daughter of Judge John Harvey Maury of Port Gibson.

Benjamin and Mildred Humphreys bought a small tract of land near Roebuck Lake in Sunflower County, cleared the land of its virgin timber, built a home and named it "Itta Bena" from the Choctaw phrase meaning "Home in the Woods." It was the first inland cotton plantation established in that swampy region. They were at Itta Bena when the war began and, although opposed to secession as a Whig, Benjamin Humphreys organized a company known as "The Sunflower Guards" and was elected their captain.

The Sunflower Guards became part of the famous 21st regiment of Mississippi Infantry and Benjamin Grubb Humphreys became colonel of the 21st. His regiment was assigned to Brig. Gen. William Barksdale's brigade of McLaw's division, Longstreet's Corps, Army of Northern Virginia and was engaged in almost every major battle. They were conspicuous in the Seven Days Battle around Richmond, Antietam, Fredericksburg, Chancellorsville, and at Gettysburg where General Humphreys assumed command of the brigade upon the death of General Barksdale as they battled for control of little round top.

Humphreys was then promoted to the rank of brigadier general as of August 12, 1863, and General Humphreys' brigade of Mississippians consisting of the thirteenth, seventeenth, eighteenth, and twenty first regiments went west with Longstreet's corps to again fight gallantly at Chickamauga, Knoxville, then in the Wilderness campaign, Spotsylvannia and Cold Harbor. His brigade reinforced Jubal Early's corps in the Shenandoah Valley campaign and eventually to Berryville, Virginia, where General Humphreys was brutally wounded, taking a minie ball in the chest, incapacitating him for further field duty. After some recuperation and not wanting to relinquish his service, he was assigned to duty with the State of Mississippi, commanding the Southern Military District where he served the remaining months of the war.

The Port Gibson contingent of war veterans riding the train to Grand Gulf in December,1882, to escort the body of their commander reminisced about many of the events of General Humphreys war feats, but also certainly remembered his unique and historic service after the war. As the first Governor elected by Mississippians under President Andrew Johnson's reconstruction plan, Governor Benjamin Grubb Humphreys provided staunch leadership as chief executive during a period of immense social, economic and political chaos. They remembered his inaugural address which contained the statement that, ".. the issue that had split the Republic had been settled on the field of battle, a tribunal from which there was no appeal." They no doubt remembered the occasion in 1867 as a result of purported violation of the Military Reconstruction Act, Governor Humphreys was ejected from office by military force and he and his wife Mildred and their children were marched out of the Governor's Mansion between files of federal soldiers with fixed bayonets, one of the most dramatic events in the history of Mississippi, with General Adelbert Ames assuming the position of chief executive of the State.

Memories, more than enough to fill ten lifetimes, rode with these men as they approached Grand Gulf. Upon their arrival they met the inbound train from Itta Bena, loaded the casket with its draped flag onto the Port Gibson bound train, and arrived in Port Gibson at 11:00 a.m. amidst hundreds of mourners gathered at the station. The body was taken to the residence of Mrs. Harding to lie in state until the funeral at 3:00 p.m. At the hour of the funeral the procession assembled in front of the Odd Fellows Hall consisting of the Comfort's band, the Cour de Lion Asylum, Knights Templar, the Claiborne Light Artillery, a large body of Confederate veterans and Franklin lodge No. 5 100F. They marched to Main street, up Main to Carroll, and thence to Farmer street to the residence of Mrs. Harding. The casket was placed on a horse drawn carriage, followed by Mildred and the family, and proceeded to the Methodist Church which was packed with mourners. The funeral began with the choir singing "Come Ye Disconsolate" after which Reverend Mr. Ballard read the funeral service of the Methodist Church of which General Humphreys had been a member for over forty years. The choir then sang "Nearer my God to Thee" and the Reverend D. A. Plauck delivered the hour long eulogy. Mr. Ballard then closed the service and as the choir sang "I Would Not Live Always," the funeral cortege reformed and proceeded to the beauty of Wintergreen Cemetery where General Humphreys was laid to his final rest.

The funeral eulogy of Reverend Plauck contained the following passage:

"By nature he was singularly fitted as an official soldier. He had courage without impetuosity; fidelity without ambition; and firmness without oppression, each soldier was his brother, and not one should suffer when it was in his power to furnish relief. He participated in nearly all the hard fought battles of the war, coming out of one having had two horses shot from under him, and with nine bullet holes through his cloak within a radius of eleven inches from his collar button, and finally returned to the conflict bearing in his body four severe wounds that undermined his health and doubtless hastened his death.

Other swords may be sheathed in scabbards of greater renown, but none in higher forms of valor and patriotism than his."

The Port Gibson Southern Reveille of that day contained the following statement about the burial.

"They buried him in the land he loved—in Dixie land—and just as the sorrowing people were retiring from the hero's grave, the setting sun went down behind his native hills, as if to veil its face and say; 'I have seen an end to all perfection.'

Servant of God well done
Rest from thy loved employ;
The battle fought, the victory won
Enter thy Master's joy."

As the family members left the grave site that afternoon surely Barnes Humphreys remembered his father's final words as he lay on his death bed in Itta Bena; "My son, whenever you meet any of my old brigade, speak to them for me."

Governor Humphreys and First Lady Mildred lie under this beautiful stone in the peaceful Wintergreen Cemetery.

FRIENDSHIP CEMETERY
COLUMBUS

Lt. Gen. Stephen Dill Lee
Brig. Gen. William Edwin Baldwin
Brig. Gen. Jacob Hunter Sharp

The muffled drum's sad roll has beat
The soldier's last tattoo!
No more on life's parade shall meet
The brave and fallen few.
On Fame's eternal camping ground
Their silent tents are spread,
And glory guards with solemn round
The bivouac of the dead.

No rumor of the foe's advance
Now swells upon the wind,
Nor troubled thought of midnight haunts,
Of loved ones left behind;
No vision of the morrow's strife
The warrior's dreams alarms,
No braying horn or screaming fife
At dawn to call to arms.

Their shivered swords are red with rust,
Their plumed heads are bowed,
Their haughty banner, trailed in dust,
Is now their martial shroud -
And plenteous funeral tears have washed
The red stains from each brow,
And the proud forms by battle gashed
Are free from anguish now.

The neighing troop, the flashing blade,
The bugle's stirring blast,
The charge,- the dreadful cannonade,
The din and shout, are passed;
Nor war's wild notes, nor glory's peal
Shall thrill with fierce delight
Those breasts that nevermore shall feel
The rapture of the fight.

Yon marble minstrel's voiceless stone
In deathless song shall tell,
When many a vanquished year hath flown,
The story how you fell.
Nor wreck nor change, nor winter's blight,
Nor time's remorseless doom,
Can dim one ray of holy light
That gilds your glorious tomb.

Theodore O'Hara

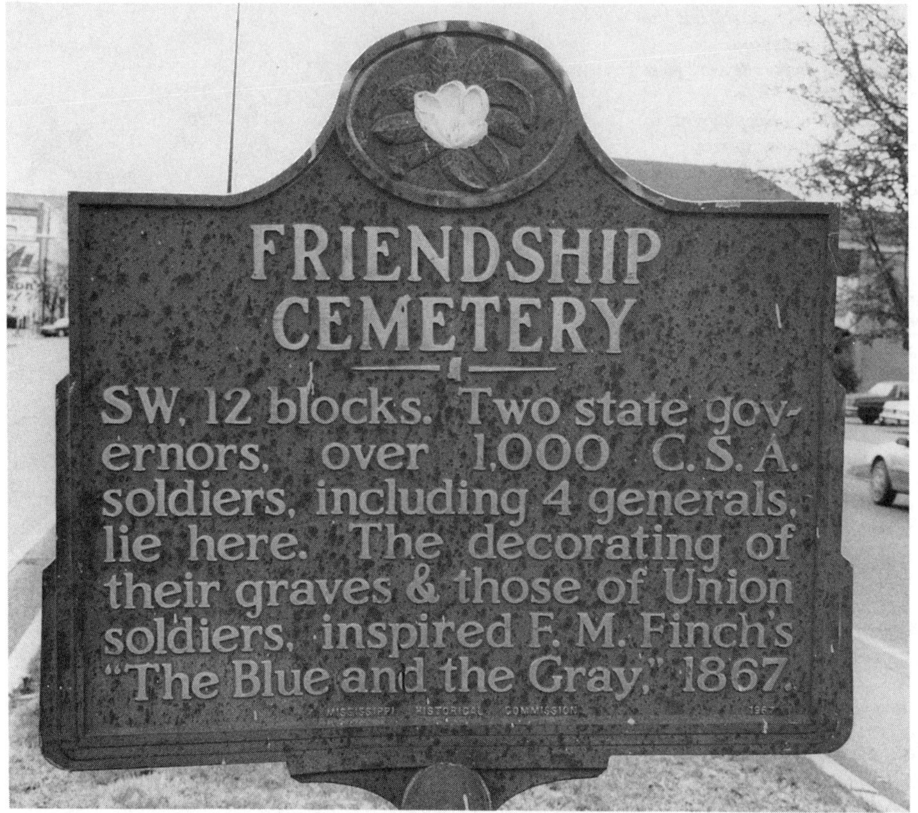

From Main Street in downtown Columbus
turn south on 4th street.

Lt. Gen. Stephen Dill Lee, C. S. A.
1833-1908

It was four o'clock, Saturday afternoon, May 30, 1908, normally the busiest day for merchants in Columbus, Mississippi, yet every store was closed voluntarily and all flags were at half mast by order of President Theodore Roosevelt. The solemn rites for one of the Confederacy's most notable corps commanders, the last remaining Confederate lieutenant general, and one of Columbus' most cherished citizens, Gen. Stephen Dill Lee, were just beginning inside the Lee home in Columbus.

The home was packed, and thousands crowded along the street of the Lee Home and down main street, black and white, awaiting the procession. There was silence. Rev. W. A. Hewitt, pastor of the First Baptist Church of Columbus of which General Lee was a prominent member, presided over the services and an impassioned eulogy was delivered by Gen. Clement A. Evans of Georgia who served in the Army of Northern Virginia under Stonewall Jackson and was himself wounded five times in the war. The choir sang "Nearer My God to Thee" and selections were read from Matthew XXV and Corinthians XV. Mrs. Harry Dashiell of Columbus sang "Face to Face" and "We Shall Meet at the River." Then the solid black casket draped with a beautiful silk Confederate Flag was carried from the home by Allen Lassiter,

Arthur Dunn, Will Waggener, Jr., Green Waggener, Guy Stuart, Walter Griffith, Robert Kindle, and Ashby McCowan, all members of the Vicksburg Southron honor guard, and placed on a horse-drawn gun carriage. The funeral procession slowly marched to Friendship Cemetery in the following order: The Mississippi A&M College Band, The George Rifles, The Lee Guards, A&M Cadet battalion, The Columbus Riflemen, Pall Bearers, Hearse, Members of family in carriages, citizens in carriages.

At the grave site, the flag was folded, three volleys were fired by the militia, taps were played, and at 6:15 p.m. the body of the beloved soldier was lowered into the grave in the family plot near the remains of other soldiers who lost their lives in the great Civil War and in a cemetery which now contains the bodies of warriors from every war from the Revolution to Vietnam.

General Lee had traveled to Vicksburg a few days earlier to address the reunion of Lawler's brigade, composed of one Wisconsin and three Iowa regiments. It was hot in the military park and after delivering a touching and eloquent speech that stirred the hearts of the old Union troops, General Lee posed for a photograph at the Iowa monument with Gen. B. B. Stevens of Wisconsin and Gen. Harvey Graham, who had once been a prisoner of General Lee. He became overheated and asked photographer Jack Moore to please hurry as he felt badly and wished to return to his quarters. Later, after eating a hearty supper he suffered an acute attack of indigestion, collapsed and after being attended by Dr. J. A. K. Birchett was taken to the home of Capt. William T. Rigby. He normally stayed at the home of Capt. Rigby when he went to Vicksburg because they were close friends. Capt. Rigby ironically was a second lieutenant in one of the companies of the 24th Iowa regiment during the siege of Vicksburg which directly faced opposite General Lee's troops during the siege of Vicksburg. After rallying briefly on Tuesday his condition began to worsen and the old warrior submitted his famed and highly lauded life at six o'clock Thursday morning, May 28, 1908. At his bedside were his brother-in-law, James T. Harrison, and his sister Mrs. Mary Harrison. His only son, Blewett Harrison Lee, general counsel for the Illinois Central Railroad in Chicago, was enroute but unable to arrive prior to the General's death.

General Lee ordered the first shot fired in the Civil War, having been one of two officers dispatched by Gen. P. G. T. Beauregard at Fort Sumter, South Carolina, to request the surrender of Major Anderson and the Fort. Upon Major Anderson's refusal, Capt. Stephen Dill Lee gave the order to the nearest battery to commence firing and this nation's costliest war was in progress. Born in Charleston, South Carolina, he was a graduate of West Point, class of 1854, and served notably in the fourth artillery regiment of the U. S. Army. He resigned his commission in 1861 to join the Confederate forces.

They Sleep Beneath the Mockingbird

After Fort Sumter, Lee participated with distinction in the battle of Seven Pines, was given command of the fourth Virginia cavalry, rendered conspicuous service at Second Manassas where as Colonel of artillery, Jefferson Davis said "he saved the day." At Antietem, where America suffered its bloodiest day in the history of all its wars, a Union counter attack on his artillery batteries threatened to overrun his position and capture the valuable pieces as his men were retreating. He hastily assembled his troops and exclaimed;

"You have this day been where men only dare to go. Some of your company have been killed; many have been wounded. But recollect it is a soldier's fate to die. Now, every man who is willing to return to the field step two paces to the front."

The men came forward, re-manned their guns, delivered a strong barrage and regained the field.

He confronted Gen. William Tecumseh Sherman at Chickasaw Bayou and with only 2,700 men repulsed Sherman's 32,000 and forced him to withdraw, losing only 207 men to Sherman's 2,700. General Lee was wounded at Champion Hill and had three horses shot from under him. He commanded the second brigade, Stevenson's division, during the siege of Vicksburg and at its fall was captured and exchanged shortly thereafter. Gen. Stephen Dill Lee was promoted to the rank of Lieutenant General at age 30, becoming the youngest lieutenant general in the Confederacy, and was given command of the Department of Mississippi, Alabama, East Louisiana, and West Tennessee. Later he assumed command of Hood's Corps near Atlanta. He won praise as he stood his ground and kept command nine hours after he was wounded at Nashville, his rear guard actions allowing the beaten southern army to escape. He surrendered and was paroled with Gen. Joseph Johnston in North Carolina on April 18, 1865.

President Jefferson Davis cherished Stephen Dill Lee. Not long before Davis' death at Beauvoir, when asked about his generals he remarked:

"Stephen D. Lee was one of the very best all-around soldiers we had. I tried him in artillery, and he handled his guns so superbly that I thought we could never spare him from that arm of the service. I tried him in command of cavalry, and he made such a dashing cavalryman that I thought he was born for that service; and when I put him to command infantry I found him equally as able and accomplished in that position. He was a great and good soldier."

General Lee settled in Columbus after the war and married Regina Harrison of that city. He was elected as a state senator, and in 1880 became the first President of the Agricultural and Mechanical College in Starkville, (now Mississippi State University). He resigned that position in 1899 to become a member of the newly created Vicksburg National Park Commission. At the time of his death he was the National Commander of the United Confederate Veterans of America.

After his death at the home of Captain Rigby, General Lee's body was prepared in Vicksburg and lay in state in the offices of the Vicksburg National Military Park from six o'clock on May 28, for Vicksburg citizens to pay their last respects to this gallant general. The Vicksburg Evening Post described the event as follows:

"He lay in a solid black casket, beneath the silken colors of the Stars and Bars. General Lee's expression is one of enduring peace and he seems to be gently sleeping. While his beard and hair are gray, the absence of furrows in his face and all signs of ravages of any consuming passions attest to the purity of his life - tell the story of his great manhood in spite of his strenuous career and that he is one of the makers of history... among those who viewed the General's body at the military park office were young people and babes, brought there by their parents who wanted them to know in years to come that the little ones had once viewed the noble features of the South's greatest and gentle sons."

On Friday, May 29, the body was brought to Columbus over the Mobile and Ohio Railroad. A request by Governor Noel to have the body lie in state at the State Capitol was denied by the family because of the funeral arrangements in Columbus on Saturday. The train bearing the body of General Lee arrived in Columbus at five o'clock that evening and was met at the depot by a large delegation.

The honorary pall bearers were listed as follows: Gen. Clement A. Evans, Gen. W.A. Montgomery, Gen. Irvin C. Walker, Col. W. T. Rigby, Col. J. C. Everett, Col. W. C Richards, Governor E. F. Noel, Hon. Dunbar Rowland, Hon. R. M. Kelly, Hon. A. F. Gray, Col. J. J. Hayes, Col. D. A. Hebron, J. G. Cashman, Capt. E. N. Scudder, and Maj. R. E. Nail.

At his funeral service in Columbus, the thoughts of his few remaining fellow soldiers no doubt went back to the terrible battlefields of the war as they heard Rev. W. A. Hewitt proclaim the final remarks:

"He died from home, but died in the post of duty. He had bravely met the enemy on many a hard fought field, but the greatest enemy he met was death. He met that enemy with the same courage, and won the greatest victory of his life. Thanks be to God which giveth us the victory, through our Lord Jesus Christ. *We are more than conquerors through Him that loved us.* However great the hero of war and conquering, life through Jesus Christ is greater. Almost three years ago, it was my privilege to go into Louisville on the same train with General Lee, to attend the Confederate Reunion. When our train pulled into the station we could see nothing but people. A hundred Kentucky Colonels, with brass bands and military companies, amid the flying flags and cheers of thousands of people, escorted him to his hotel and gave him the most royal welcome that Southern chivalry can accord a hero of war. But there was a more glorious welcome extended to a mightier conqueror on last Thursday morning at six o'clock when his chariot drove up to the Gates of Gold! The veterans of a glorious war, the angels and archangels and hosts of heaven came down to the gates to meet and greet this hero who was more than conqueror through Him that loved us."

In a speech given in Columbus in 1904, General Stephen Dill Lee stated:

"I state here that even we of the South would not have slavery restored. The sentiment of the world is against it and we, too, feel that way now. But let our children know that we did not fight to maintain slavery, but for constitutional rights."

General Lee's grave in Friendship Cemetery, Columbus, is covered with a concrete slab with his name engraved. It is surrounded by the graves of his family and is fenced with a bronze bust of General Lee. The family plot is located in the southeastern part of the beautiful cemetery.

Brig. Gen. William Edwin Baldwin, C. S. A.
1827-1864

The dreaded dispatch from Col. William S. Barry was hurriedly galloped by courier to Maj. D. W. Flowerree, Assistant Adjutant General of the Department of the Gulf in the early morning hours of February 20, 1864. It read as follows:

"Major: It becomes my painful duty to announce to the Major General Commanding the death of Brig. Gen. Wm. E. Baldwin. He died yesterday evening about 7 o'clock. Riding on horseback, about a mile west of Dog River, he was, by the breaking of a stirrup, thrown suddenly and violently forward, and fell upon his right shoulder. He never spoke after his fall, though he continued to live for an hour. He breathed his last just as he was borne into his quarters. Scarcely a sign of violence was found upon his person, and the terrible result is supposed by the Surgeon to have been produced by a violent concussion of the brain."

It was a terrible personal loss for Colonel Barry since they had been boyhood friends back in Columbus, Mississippi. But the members of the brigade also deeply felt the loss of their leader whom they had followed through the capture of Fort Donelson, the siege of Vicksburg and many other battles. Except for wounds at Donelson and Vicksburg, General Baldwin had arrived at Mobile, Alabama in early

1864, relatively unscathed although having fought in many fierce engagements. He shared the indigenous talents of most all southern reared men of the day, expert horsemanship. As was once noted by Col. R. W. Banks;

"...it should be kept in mind that in those days nearly every Mississippian was accustomed from youth to horse and gun and outdoor life. Nearly all of them, old and young, engaged in those exciting athletic sports which develop familiarity with firearms and compel bold riding which Macauley says 'has been called the image of war.' Such activities qualified men for camp and they were indulged in by well nigh every mother's son in every state of the south."

A true military leader and horseman he was, but William Edwin Baldwin also had a rare affinity for books. Back in Columbus before the war he operated a book and stationery store and took every opportunity to familiarize himself with the content of books on almost any subject in print. He wanted to go back there when the war was over and return to the serene enjoyment of his friends and books.

William Edwin Baldwin was born in Sumter District, South Carolina on August 27, 1827, and moved with his family to Columbus at a very early age. There, as a young man in 1845, he became a member of Captain Abert's "Columbus Rifles" and was soon elected their first lieutenant. With the beginning of the Civil War, the "Columbus Rifles" elected Baldwin captain on May 23, 1861, and they departed for service in Pensacola, Florida. Very soon they were grouped with the "Shubuta Infantry," the "Enterprise Guards," the "Quitman Invincibles," the "Beauregard Rifles," and the "Meridian Invincibles" to form the 14th Mississippi Regiment with William Edwin Baldwin as their colonel.

By early 1862, Colonel Baldwin was commanding a brigade and was engaged in the defense of Fort Donelson, in Tennessee. He was captured along with his brigade at the surrender of the fort and was imprisoned at Fort Warren, Massachusetts until August, 1862. Upon his exchange he was promoted to brigadier general, effective September 19, 1862, and by December was again in front of his brigade at Coffeeville, Mississippi aiding immensely in checking General Grant's first advance toward Vicksburg and receiving laudatory reference from General Tilghman in his report;

"I take special pleasure in mentioning the name of Brig. Gen. W. E. Baldwin, of my own division.... displayed the greatest good judgment and gallantry."

Later at Port Gibson, Bayou Pierre, Champion Hill, and the Big Black he led his brigade in battle before falling back into defensive positions at Vicksburg where he was wounded a second time and became a prisoner upon the fall of the city on July

4, 1863. He spent most of his incarceration at Enterprise, Mississippi, was exchanged, took his brigade to Dalton, Georgia in the fall of 1863 and then to Mobile in early 1864 where the final tragedy happened.

Gen. Claudius Sears who was present at the time of General Baldwin's death wrote in his diary;

Feb. 19. "In Mobile with Gen. Baldwin. Met Henry Addison and with him called upon his sister, Mrs. Baltre- remained at dog River During February, on the 19th Feb. 1864, Gen. Baldwin was killed, running his horse at a furious rate, stumbled and broke the General's neck - too much whiskey in the crowd. Col W. S. Barry 35th Ms. regiment assumed command as being senior Col."

One of the soldiers (Chambers) of General Baldwin's command entered the following passage in his diary on the 20th of February, recorded in <u>My Journal-Chambers:</u>

"..was overcast with clouds, and a strong north wind was blowing. About 3 o'clock P.M. snow began to fall which continued till after dark. There is gloom over our camp today. Gen. Baldwin is dead! That proud dashing form is cold and stiff in death—the light in those eagle eyes is gone out, and the splendid mind has ceased to exist so far as we are concerned. A few hours since, Brig. Gen. Wm. E. Baldwin seemed a favorite of fortune. He was in the prime of life, blessed with health, riches, and honor, respected by his soldiers and confided in by his superiors, the path of preferment seemed to be already open before him.
Monday, Feb., 22 ....Gen. Baldwin's remains were buried yesterday. I think nearly the entire Brigade attended the funeral, only one regiment bearing arms. (The funeral procession of the General of Brigade is one regiment of Infantry, a Company of Cavalry, and two pieces of artillery, though as many others as wish to, can join the procession, carrying only side arms.)"

Although General Baldwin was initially interred at Dog River Factory, Alabama, he was later disinterred and transported by train back home to Columbus where he was laid to his final resting place in Friendship Cemetery in the town where his parents, sisters and wife resided. The weary stirrup that failed him during a strong run of his horse cruelly abbreviated the life of a gallant soldier, model citizen, lover of books and arts, friend to all, brave defender of the Confederacy, and hero of Columbus.

General Baldwin's grave stone in Friendship Cemetery marks the spot where his remains were re-interred after the war. It stands north of the Confederate grave sites and is near the center of the cemetery.

Brig. Gen. Jacob Hunter Sharp, C. S. A.
1833-1907

On the warm and muggy summer night of September 16, 1907, seventy-four year old Confederate warrior, General "Jake" Sharp, lay on his deathbed in his Columbus, Mississippi, home. It was approaching midnight and his final struggle had begun. Along with a few close friends at his bedside were his wife of almost fifty years, Sallie Harris Sharp, and his son Capt. T. H. Sharp, who had seen duty in the Spanish American War.

For the preceding few years, because of his failing health, Jake Sharp was seldom seem on the streets of Columbus, but even though out of sight of his many friends and fellow veterans, he was still very much in their hearts and minds. Some fondly remembered him as an effectual attorney, owner and editor of their local newspaper "The Columbus Independent," President of the Mississippi Press Association, Speaker of the Mississippi House of Representatives, and model citizen. But all revered him for his unforgettable contributions on the fields of battle during the war between the states. Gen. Stephen Dill Lee, his former Corps commander and fellow Columbian had recently reminded the Mississippi Legislature of the daring exploits of their former Speaker of the House:

"He led his command through the famous "locust thicket" (Battle of Franklin, Tennessee) that ordinarily a dog could not have gotten through; he led them to the breast works of the enemy and engaged in a death struggle over them, the troops on each side bayoneting each other. He captured three stands of colors, the only Confederate trophies taken on the ensanguined field. He was equally gallant on other fields; but if there was none other but Franklin, his name should go down immortal in history as a hero who led a band of Mississippians, all of whom were heroes."

General Sharp was born in Pickens County Alabama, February 6, 1833, moving to Lowndes County, Mississippi at an early age. He attended Feemster's private school in the Caledonia neighborhood, later the University of Alabama, and studied law under Judge William L. Harris in Columbus. He was admitted to the bar and later married the Judge's daughter Sallie, and began his practice with his brother Thomas I. Sharp in Columbus. The Sharp brothers were very close.

As described by their friend Col. R. W. Banks of Columbus;

"They were young men of easy fortune, both were well educated and excellent types of the southern manhood composing the Confederate specimens of the Mississippi volunteer soldiers, whose virtue and valor and patriotic performances on every field whose dangers they shared added to the renown of the state and made the world ring anew with praise of the prowess of her sons.... Jake was not dissolute or given to reckless dissipation; was more inclined to be a rollicking blade—fun-loving and festive. In disposition he was less a roundhead than a cavalier... however he was high-spirited and ardent, and would have considered a display of lack of courage on any field as a dishonor more to be shunned than death."

As was the case in many families throughout the country the outbreak of the Civil War in 1861 parted the two brothers forever. Jake enlisted as a private in the "Tombigbee Rangers" in February, 1861, which later became Company A of the 44th Mississippi Infantry. Tom enlisted in the "Southern Avengers" in March forming as company E of the 10th Mississippi Infantry. Fate dealt them a very different hand as Jake rose through the ranks from private to brigadier general and Tom as a captain was killed on the field at Ezra Church near Atlanta.

Jacob Hunter Sharp saw action early in the war. His regiment was heavily engaged at Belmont, then at Shiloh where their commander, Colonel A. K Blythe was killed and Jake Sharp took over. They fought at Munfordville and Murfreesboro, then at Chickamauga where Sharp was made colonel in 1863, and was commanding the entire brigade.

They Sleep Beneath the Mockingbird

Gen. Braxton Bragg gave the 44th brigade the sobriquet "High Pressure Brigade" since they seemed to always be in the thick of every fight, Sharp providing the catalyst of strong leadership as an "up front" brigade commander. They were made up of the 7th, 9th, 41st Mississippi Infantry and the 9th battalion of sharpshooters. The flag bearer of the 44th brigade wrote of General Sharp in 1902:

"He was one of the most gallant souls that ever wore a Confederate officer's uniform. In my imagination I often see him on his little cream-colored pony at the head of the brigade. He was an inspiration of himself to the entire brigade."

At Jonesboro, Georgia, division commander Gen. Patton Anderson described their fighting:

"From the defenses, the enemy poured an unrelenting fire upon the assailants. Though at a distance from them, Sharp's gallant Mississippians could be seen pushing their way up the very slope of the enemy's breastworks. The 44th lost within one-half of its entire number. Officers could be plainly observed encouraging the men to their work. One on horseback, whom I took to be General Sharp, was particularly conspicuous."

At Resaca, Georgia, Sharp was promoted to brigadier general on the field succeeding Gen. W. F. Tucker who was disabled by wounds. Then at Franklin, Tennessee, General Sharp's "High Pressure Brigade" of Stephen Dill Lee's Corps was called upon to deliver the "locust grove", a point of the stiffest union resistance, and a task that other units had failed to accomplish. It was getting late in the day and the fight for the "locust grove" continued - it was well after midnight when the fighting finished. According to George W. Leavell of Oxford, a member of the "High Pressure Brigade," "Our progress was retarded by the brush which had been cut down. We clambered, pulled through, or crawled under on hands and knees as best we could."

In another description of the action;

"Sharp's Brigade approached first, and were greeted with a volley so surely aimed that nearly half the brigade seemed to fall at once to the ground, but the survivors with a yell rushed forward to the ditch. From the trenches, parties of Mississippians would climb upon the works, tear down the flags, and raise their own, which were in turn pulled down, and the daring assailants driven back or killed. Part of Sharp's brigade could not be driven from their lodgement on the parapets, over which they kept up a fire through the night, being the first to enter Franklin when the Union withdrew the next morning."

So the "locust grove" was delivered by Gen. Jacob Hunter Sharp's "High Pressure Brigade" of Mississippians, but not until after General Sharp himself had been painfully wounded in the leg. He later wrote;

"I was shot just below the knee and it seemed as if my leg was shivered into splinters; ... at the battle of Nashville I was on crutches and on the second day's stampede I had to be helped on my horse."

The bloody fighting in Georgia, Franklin, and Nashville had reduced the "High Pressure Brigade" from 2,000 men to only 431. Although decimated, they would go on into North Carolina and after their last engagement at Bentonville, surrender at Durham Station on April 26, 1865.

General Sharp returned to his home in Columbus and practiced law with partners J. E. Leigh and Capt. W. W. Humphries. He acquired the ownership of "The Columbus Independent" and served in the Mississippi Legislature for six terms. He was elected "Speaker of the House" in 1886, and although making an unsuccessful campaign for State Treasurer, he was one of the most renowned statesmen of the day.

When he breathed his last breath just before the stroke of midnight on September 16, 1907, the City of Columbus, the State of Mississippi, and the South lost a true and devoted leader. Following his funeral which was held at the First Methodist Church at 10 A.M. on September,18, with the Rev. R. A. Clark officiating, Gen. Stephen Dill Lee delivered an emotional eulogy at his graveside in Friendship Cemetery. Members of the Isham Harrison Camp No. 27, United Confederate Veterans, many of whom served in the "High Pressure Brigade" conducted the burial as the Columbus Riflemen fired three volleys in salute.

The honorary pallbearers were; Judge J. A. Orr, E. T. Sykes, Gen. S. D. Lee, Dr. R. L. Sykes, Capt. D. Walburg, Judge Newman Cayce, Capt. D. P. Davis, and Col. W. D. Humphries. Serving as active pall bearers were: E. R. Sherman, P. W. Maer, S. S. Scales, R. T. Williams, T. W. Hardy and Walter Weaver.

In an obituary of General Sharp, Gen. Robert Lowry stated:

"To the humblest soldier from Lowndes County he was always "Jake"; to the commander of the army he was General Sharp; but at all times and under all circumstances he was the same kind, genial and gallant gentleman, beloved by officers and men alike."

General Sharp's impressive grave stone is shown above in Friendship Cemetery. In the background are rows of Confederate grave stones shaded by magnificent Magnolias.

BILOXI CEMETERY
BILOXI

Brig. Gen. Joseph Robert Davis

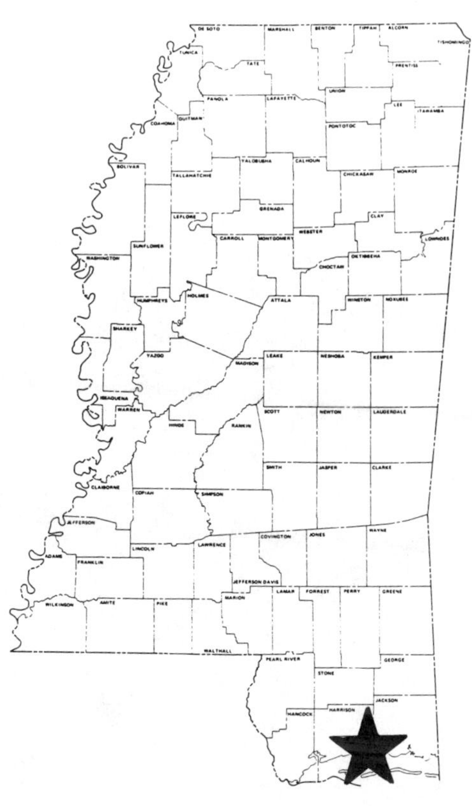

Dead he lay upon his bier;
Friends passed by and dropped a tear.
Some one said in sympathy:
"In his youth he rode with Lee."

Well he bore his part in life,
Calm amid its cares and strife,
Doing all so buoyantly;
In his youth he rode with Lee.

Things that others thought so small
Made to him a special call;
Careful, patient, faithful, he;
In his youth he rode with Lee.

Men said: "This man worketh well;
Why so hard? 'Tis hard to tell.'
Yet he worked so manfully,
For in his youth he rode with Lee.

Loved he was by hosts of friends,
Each one his good name commends,
Some forgetting, tho' not he,
That in his youth he rode with Lee.

Many years have passed since he
Rode away so merrily;
Now his people's pride shall be
That in youth he rode with Lee.

Rosewell Page

Located on the north side of highway 90
just west of Biloxi.

Brig. Gen. Joseph Robert Davis, C. S. A.
1825-1896

The Battle of Gettysburg was entering its third fateful day. The opposing forces facing each other from across an open field almost a mile apart were not the same clumsy, unorganized, and untrained bands of men who opened the conflict over two years earlier. They were highly disciplined, well accoutered, battle hardened, and tactically astute veterans, the cream of the crop of both union and confederate forces, well led and fully inspired.

Battle lines had been formed by the previous two days of bloody fighting; the Union Army of the Potomac occupying Cemetery Ridge and, across the wide expanse of open countryside, the Confederate Army of Northern Virginia was positioned along Seminary Ridge. Gen. Robert E. Lee had made a monumental decision to attack the Union center. Pickett's Charge, arguably the gallant decisive fatal surge of the Confederacy on which hinged the outcome of the war, was about to begin. Pickett's charge would forever point out the futility of advancing large numbers of troops in close order toward fixed positions of well armed opposing forces. The weaponry had exceeded the tactics.

One of the brigades forming up in the woods behind Seminary Ridge to augment Pickett's division of fresh troops was a brigade of Mississippians and North

Carolinians from Heth's division, A. P. Hill's corps under the command of Brig. Gen. Joseph Robert Davis, the nephew of President Jefferson Davis. The Davis brigade had seen heavy action on the first day of battle and their ranks had been decimated to only a thousand men, many of whom were wounded and needed medical attention. Now they were about to join more than eleven thousand other Confederate soldiers in an advance across an open field and into the pages of history. They were the "University Grays" from "Ole Miss," the "Calhoun Rifles," "Iuka Rifles," "Chickasaw Rifles," "Noxubee Troopers," "Carroll Rifles," "Tishomingo Rifles," and tens of other companies with names just as proud, all Mississippians except for the regiment of North Carolinians and they were ready, even though battered. They would form the second brigade from the left end of the line flanked only by a brigade of Virginians on their left. Just prior to the artillery barrage which would preface the charge, Gen. Robert E. Lee called General Davis, and the other brigade commanders along with the division commander, General Pickett, together and went over the details of the attack. With the plan of attack understood by all, the commanders went back to their units to await the appointed hour. The decision was now irreversible.

When the artillery barrage ceased, the augmented division of General Pickett moved forward from the woods and formed up on the edge of the field. The stifling smoke from the artillery in the 90 degree temperature along with the apprehension of what was to come made it extremely difficult, but the men formed up as if in dress parade and along the left side of the formation stood General Davis and his brigade. As General Lee noticed the weakened state of the Mississippi brigade, his eyes swelled with tears and he remarked, "they shouldn't be here." But they had already been chosen and they were ready to fight again. The order was given to advance, and thrusting forward in "route step" they began the fateful venture. The Mississippians were in one of the most exposed positions but did not receive hostile fire until they had advanced about one-quarter mile, whereupon the Union artillery began to come in heavy, taking out scores of men with each volley. On they marched, reforming after every explosion into their ranks and maintaining superb discipline. They began to receive canister from Union artillery. Then as they crossed Emmitsburg road the Union riflemen opened up in enfilade cutting them down like hay. They continued on, reforming as they went, even though the Virginians on their immediate left under the command of Col. John M. Brockenbrough stopped and began to fall back in confusion and disarray leaving General Davis' brigade as the extreme left anchor of Pickett's Charge. As their numbers grew smaller men began to bunch up into small groups and continue toward the deadly fire. Only about a dozen ever reached the stone wall behind which the Union Army was delivering fire and there they were immediately killed or captured. The rest had fallen wounded or staggered backwards, their fronts facing the enemy, in shock and dismay.

They Sleep Beneath the Mockingbird

General Lee rode onto the field where the dazed soldiers were returning in front of the wood line at seminary ridge and told them it was all his fault and requested they reform to defend against a possible Union counter attack. When the brigade reformed behind Seminary Ridge after the battle, General Davis wept openly as he counted only a handful of his men remaining. The University Grays took 100 percent casualties, and the rest of his units in excess of 80 percent.

In the weeks and months following Pickett's charge General Davis reformed and reconstituted his brigade. Fighting on, they asserted their presence at the Battle of the Wilderness, Spotsylvania, Cold Harbor, Richmond and Petersburg. Gen. Joe Davis and his men stood in prideful formation at Appomattox Court House and surrendered along with the rest of the Army of Northern Virginia. They had seen some of the most terrible battles of the war.

Gen. Joseph R. Davis served on the staff of President Jefferson Davis at the opening of the Civil War but opted for the field and was subsequently given a command. Although having no formal military training he followed in the footsteps of his father, Isaac Davis, an officer in Andrew Jackson's command during the war of 1812, and who displayed gallantry at Fort Mims. His grandfather, Samuel Emory Davis, fought fearlessly in the ranks during the Revolutionary War. Born in Wilkinson County in 1825, Joe Davis became a planter, lawyer, and legislator in Mississippi prior to the war, with a most genial and sociable personality. He returned after the war to practice law spending most of his career on the Mississippi Gulf Coast, becoming one of Biloxi's most celebrated and respected citizens.

Death came to the gallant warrior not in the terrible clash of battle, but peacefully at age 71, on a warm Tuesday evening, September 15, 1896, at 7:30, at his home after battling a kidney ailment for many months. His loving wife, Margaret Cary Greene, a descendant of Gen. Nathaniel Greene, of Rhode Island, and their two daughters Varina and Edith by were by his bedside. Amidst an extremely large gathering of mourners, Gen. Joseph Robert Davis was buried in the beautiful Biloxi Cemetery on September 16, at 5 o'clock p.m. The cemetery is located near the site of the earliest French settlement on the Gulf Coast.

The Biloxi Herald on September 19, 1896, published the following obituary of General Davis:

"Completing and even going beyond the Psalmist's allotment of days of man, from his earliest youth, through all of his manhood's years and down to the day of his death, he lived loyally by those precepts of honor and truth that were the distinguishing characteristics of the men of the ancient regime in the South, and he '...ever bore without reproach the grand old name of gentlemen.' No modern gospel of expediency could tempt his feet away from the path of principle and the things he thought worth living for, in his esteem, were worth dying for too. He gave his life's service to the affirmation of a high ideal and his record cannot fail to be an inspiration to the youth of Mississippi. It proves that honor must come to those who live an honorable life, and that all honor must follow a devoted service of right. General Davis never said or wrote one word that did not have conscientious conviction behind it, and, for this reason, his fellow citizens loved and trusted him."

The grave site of General Davis is located in the southwest quadrant of the Old Biloxi Cemetery, just off highway 90, overlooking the Gulf of Mexico.

HILL CREST CEMETERY
HOLLY SPRINGS

Maj. Gen. Edward Cary Walthall
Brig. Gen. Winfield Scott Featherston
Brig. Gen. Samuel Benton
Brig. Gen. Daniel Chevilette Govan

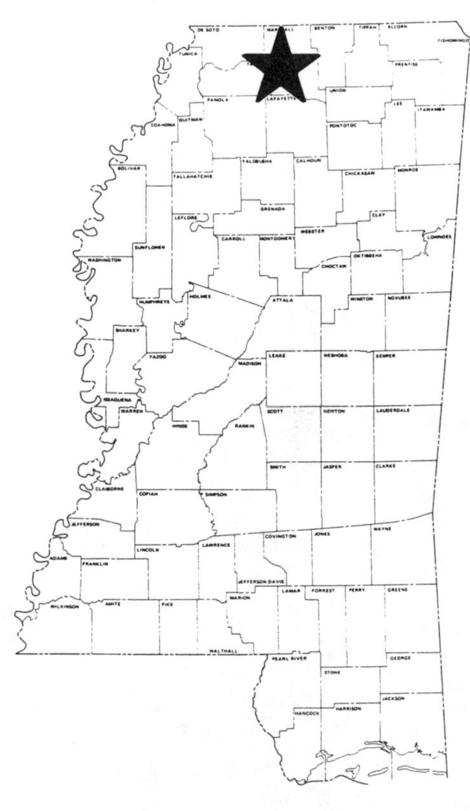

Do they love you still in Dixie?
Ah, how they love you still!
The deathless courage of your lives
Make every true heart thrill
And beat with loving warmth and pride
At deeds so nobly done;
So shall it be throughout the years
Till quick and dead are one.

Do they love you still in Dixie?
Ah, could you have a doubt
That Dixie sons of Dixie sires
Would ever turn about
And worship at a lesser shrine
Than that you raised so high?
Its matchless glory cannot wane,
Its stars yet pierce the sky.

Do they love you still in Dixie?
Ah, can they e'er forget
How nobly strove those ranks of gray
When Hope's fair sun had set,
And bleeding died their cause to save,
Nor dying won the day,
Though cause more just man ne'er has known
Or deadlier yet the fray?

Yes, we love you still in Dixie!
You and your sweethearts, too,
For your sweethearts are our mothers-
Can you doubt that we are true?
Though your ranks now fast are melting
And the Stars and Bars are furled,
Yet the South will live forever
In the glory of your world.

Emmet Rodwell Calhoun

Hill Crest Cemetery is located three blocks south of the town square on Market Street.

Maj. Gen. Edward Cary Walthall, C. S. A.
1831-1898

It was a somber occasion in the United States Capitol on April 23, 1898. The body of one of the most respected and beloved U. S. Senators of that era, Edward Cary Walthall, had just been brought into the Senate Chamber. It was exactly 12 o'clock when Vice President Garret Hobart called the Senate to order. The members of the House of Representatives then proceeded into the chamber escorted by the Sergeant at Arms and the Clerk and headed by the Speaker and Chaplain. They were followed by the members of the diplomatic corps, the Chief Justice and members of the Supreme Court, President William McKinley and his cabinet along with the family and many friends of Senator Walthall. After the service and eulogies given by many of his colleagues, his casket was borne from the Senate Chamber by pallbearers selected from the Capitol police, placed on a carriage and taken to Union Station where it was placed aboard a special funeral train bound for Holly Springs, Mississippi. Just two weeks earlier, General Walthall had risen from his sick bed in very frail condition to come to the Senate and deliver a stirring memorial address on behalf of the memory of his deceased longtime friend and fellow statesman Senator James Z. George, the "Old Commoner."

When the black draped funeral trained crossed into Mississippi bound for its destination, mourners were gathered at every station. As the train stopped at each one they came aboard to pay their respects to the man they loved so dearly. They were the humble and the great, black and white. Many brought wild flowers gathered from fence corners and tearfully placed them at the foot of his coffin. At the Holly Springs depot there was a mass gathering including almost everyone in town, but especially touching was a contingent of aging Confederate Veterans, members of Camp Kit Mott, many of whom served with him in battle and who never left the side of the coffin until it was lowered into the ground. The cadets from St. Thomas Hall where he attended school formed the honor guard along with the Grenada Rifles of the National Guard as the procession proceeded to Christ Church in Holly Springs. At 2:00 p.m. the funeral service was conducted by Bishop Thompson, Rev. Stephen Greene and P. G. Seers. The active pall bearers were Governors Stone and Lowry, George M. Govan, James Longstreet, Ben Adams, William Strickland, Addison Craft, J. C. Kyle, R. H. Henry, and R. W. Banks.

No doubt the Confederate Veterans of the Walthall brigade were reminiscing of many raging battles in which General Walthall placed himself in front of the regiment and faced withering fire to lead them on. His units were usually given hard assignments and placed in the thick of every fight because of his bravery and his motivation of his men. At Chickamauga he lost nearly one third of his men and had only 600 battered soldiers left for the " battle above the clouds" on Lookout Mountain but bravely covered the retreat of the Confederate Army on Missionary Ridge the next day. He was severely wounded in the foot in that battle and refused to leave the field until his men had withdrawn, then was so fatigued that he had to be helped from the saddle. General Walthall led his men with distinction in the fighting around Atlanta. He was in the midst of the bloody battle at Franklin, Tennessee, where he led his men across the open plain before the Federal parapets under fire described by many as the heaviest they had ever seen in the war and where eleven southern generals fell. He had two horses shot from under him during this charge. Gen. John Bell Hood chose Walthall to augment Gen. Nathan Bedford Forrest's cavalry (at Forrest's request) in covering the retreat of his army from Tennessee, a daring feat which required extremely heroic and intense rear guard actions.

Although usually outnumbered by a large margin his men always acquitted themselves well though suffering heavy losses. Military historians often rank Major General Walthall second only to Nathan Bedford Forrest in the Army of the Tennessee. Gen. Joseph E. Johnston remarked that Walthall would have been given command of all the Confederate armies in the western division if the war had continued a year longer.

At the dedication of the Mississippi Confederate Monument which now stands in front of the Archives and History building in Jackson, General Walthall made an unforgettable speech to the twenty five thousand who had assembled to honor the State's Confederate dead. Walthall's words that day included the following:

" We did not go to war for slavery, though slavery was woven with the causes, and intensified the bitterness of the war, and the fate of slavery was forever settled by the result. We were not precipitated into it by reckless public men who had not counted the cost, for the great leaders, and notably Mr. Davis, were slower in the movements than the masses of southern people. We did not take up arms because we were dissatisfied with our form of government, for we valued that then as we value it now; and we so loved the constitution for the safeguards of liberty which we read in it, that we fashioned our confederated constitution after it as a model. We loved the flag, too, with its stars telling of co-equal states in a common union, so long as it floated above us with that symbolism. Happily it now floats over us again, as the full equals of all who live under its protection. The war, with us, did not originate in ambition, nor did we fight for spoils, for conquest or for fame. With us it was no war of invasion or of revenge. It was not to build up some great leader's fortunes nor to elevate some popular favorite to place or power. We went to war for none of these; but it was 'to save the constitution,' as we read it, and to save ourselves and to preserve our cherished form of government. We resisted those perversions which we believed would destroy that constitution and us, and subvert that form of government. ....it was the effort to establish the true boundary line between the constitutional authority and the state and the general government that brought the war upon us. It was to maintain the theory of government which Mr. Calhoun and those of his school taught us, that 600,000 southern soldiers went eagerly to the field, and they, to whom we raise this monument freely gave up their lives. It was not for power, nor for riches, nor for ambition's sake, but for a great governmental principle of right, which was rooted and grounded in their faith and sanctioned by their judgments. Without faltering or wavering our martyred dead stood by this principle with their lives and while the great guns of war shook to its center this now peaceful and prosperous land, while men were slain by tens of thousands and hearts were stricken and homes were darkened, while the groans of the dying and the wails of those bereft burdened the very air from Maryland to the Rio Grande, inspired by their example those who survived stood to the last by the teachings of Calhoun and Davis and those who held the same political faith. ....we have the memories of these martyrs to cherish, and revere, we have our 'consecrated coronet of sorrow,' and we have the image of the confederate soldier which he has graven upon the tablets of history to tell our story for us, and we are content."

General Walthall was district attorney for the tenth district of Mississippi at the outbreak of the War. His family had moved to Mississippi from his birthplace of Richmond, Virginia in 1841. He loved Mississippi dearly, and practiced law at Coffeeville and Grenada. He became a stabilizing force in the aftermath of the war and was instrumental along with Lamar, George, Harris, Featherston, and others in overthrowing carpetbag rule in Mississippi. He was appointed to the United States Senate in 1885 to fill the vacancy of L. Q. C. Lamar. He never ran for public office, being a four term United States Senator without becoming a candidate, he was always called by the people into public service.

Perhaps John Sharp Williams eulogized him best when he said:

"He was almost the last of a long line of Mississippians of historic type and fame. The old historic ideals about which the Southern life revolved ......is they say, losing its molding force. They say something better will take its place. I do not believe it... It has lost its force with this generation in a measure, though not altogether. The transition stage from an old to a new industrial life has partially destroyed that, as it has destroyed many other sweet flowers, which will, however, spring afresh to bloom anew among the beauties of the new order, fertilized by the ashes of the old."

When Maj. Gen. Edward Cary Walthall was laid to rest in the serenity of Hillcrest Cemetery in Holly Springs in April, 1898, amidst thousands of mourners, the surrounding floral and fragrant emergence of springtime was fitting for the man who in his short sixty-seven years of life on this earth blossomed so fully and completely, a unique blossom the likes of which we may not observe again.

Stately monument above the grave of Senator Walthall in family plot in Hill Crest Cemetery.

Brig. Gen. Winfield Scott Featherston, C. S. A.
1820-1891

His men affectionately called him "old Swet." He was a hard driver and merciless fighter, a characteristic obtained as a seventeen year old combatant in the Creek Indian Wars of the 1830's, and certainly characteristic of his namesake, Winfield Scott of the War of 1812, and the Mexican War. Scott Featherston came from a Georgia family of wealth and influence. The youngest of seven children, he obtained a good education, attending academies in Columbus, Georgia, and law school in Memphis, Tennessee. By the time he settled into his successful law practice in Houston, Mississippi, in 1840, at the age of nineteen, he was an able stump speaker, fluent and well informed in political history, and lauded with military notoriety. Featherston parlayed these assets into a seat in the United States Congress in 1847 and was re-elected in 1849. In 1857, he continued his practice of law, moving to Holly Springs, and was Mississippi's Commissioner to Kentucky on secession matters in 1860.

When the civil war began, Winfield Scott Featherston was one of the first to answer the call to service. He recruited a company which was mustered into the 17th Mississippi infantry and was elected their colonel. They were the "Sam Benton Rifles," "Mississippi Rangers," "Burnsville Blues," "Panola Vindicators," and "Magnolia Guards," and they saw action very early. By October 1861 they were in

Leesburg, in Northern Virginia when Union forces under the command of Col. Edward Baker, attempted to dislodge the Confederate forces from their position forty miles upriver from Washington. Colonel Featherston led a violent charge into the federals which resulted in the death of Colonel Baker and the loss of over half of his 1,700 men as the Union regiment was forced over a one hundred foot cliff and into the Potomac River. Upon being informed of this action President Lincoln was brought to tears at the loss of his close personal friend, Colonel Baker, and the tragic defeat of his force during this action which became known as the Battle of Ball's Bluff.

Featherston was soon promoted to brigadier general in Army of Northern Virginia and continued to command his Mississippians throughout most of the battles of that theater including the siege of Yorktown, the Peninsula Campaign, Gaines Mill, the second Battle of Manassas and Fredericksburg. His brigade included the 12th, 16th, 19th, and 48th Mississippi regiments.

At his own request he was dispatched to the Western front, to the defense of Vicksburg. They were too late to prevent the Union encirclement of the city but skillfully evaded capture when the city capitulated and continued to fight throughout the state. Then there were the memorable campaigns in Georgia where his brigade of Mississippians helped resist the advance of Gen. William Tecumseh Sherman. At Peachtree Creek, July 20, 1864, Featherston advanced his 1,230 men against the breastworks of the Union defense and lost 616 brave soldiers. Throughout the Tennessee campaign with General Hood they fearlessly fought on, in the destructive battles of Franklin and Nashville, and to the final surrender in North Carolina.

The war did not end the battles of Winfield Scott Featherston. He returned to his favored city, Holly Springs, and continued his practice of law and civil service. He served as a legislator and circuit judge and in 1876, conducted the impeachment proceedings against Governor Adelbert Ames who resigned during the process. Featherston was encouraged and supported by many to run for Governor. He was a member of the Constitutional Convention of 1890 and was elected as Grand Commander of the Confederate Veterans of the State, an office he enjoyed until his death.

Winfield Scott Featherston's death came quietly at 8:50 p.m. on Thursday, May 28, 1891, in his 72nd year, at his residence in Holly Springs, the result of paralysis caused by a stroke. At 4:30 on the beautiful spring afternoon of Friday, May 29, the general who had fought so many battles both in combat and as a statesman was laid to rest in lovely Hill Crest Cemetery, with the Reverend T. W. Raymond officiating. The newspaper description of the interment contained the following:

"The old veterans who had seen him in his might and strength, and had followed him who knew no fear, where death was reaping a rich harvest, followed the helpless clay to its last resting place with tearful eyes and solemn step; the muffled drums and funeral march remind them of the vanity of earthly honors. A sorrowful multitude of all classes and conditions surrounded his grave. They had left their various avocations to do the last honors to a man whose place will be hard to fill in our community. As a man he was brave and generous, as a friend he could hardly be excelled, as a public spirited citizen he was always ready with the powers of his intellect and the force of his mighty will to advocate any cause for the good of his town and country, and by the church of which he was a member and had supported liberally with his counsel and material means his loss will be deeply felt."

Five days later at a meeting of Confederate veterans, Major Craft eulogized General Featherston eloquently:

"It was a long and sorrowful procession that which formed his last escort, slowly marching to the strains of dirge-like music, but without other military insignia than the badges of the column of veterans who kept the old time step in mournful rhythm. We fired no gun over his bier. His fitting salute was heard in the echoes of the shouted salvos whose reverberations shook the many battlefields upon which his conspicuous gallantry played so important a part. But speaking from my own personal experience there was not a veteran in all that solemn cotege who failed on the way to her silent city to live over again the scenes of the camp and field: to feel within his bosom the surging of the spirit of the strife; to recall other burials where prayers were short and rites were few, and who did not realize the intimate association as incidents in the same grand historic chapter between the funeral of this eminent commander and the hasty putting out of sight the mangled forms of the hundreds of his heroic followers who went down in the shock of battle. With them lay the destiny and the glory of pouring out their life's blood in the defense of home and country upon the stricken field. To him it was given to escape the casualty of conflict, to be spared through long years to serve his State in other dire times of need, to win distinction at the bar and in the forum, to dignify the bench, to adorn the church, to endear the home and fireside, and in the fullness of years but still in the enjoyment of manly vigor to fall under a sudden summon. Yet the connecting link is ever unbroken and the newly raised mound which marks the resting place of this once general of a division is but a part of the long alignment reaching back through the years to the gorged trenches which answered for sepulchre in the days when strong columns vanished in the onset. Whether enfolding the form of officer or private whether unmarked by the wayside or strewn by loving hands with flowers and graced by stately monument there is kinship still even beneath the sod they are all the graves of the honored Confederate soldiers. It is the fraternal sentiment, old veterans as you are, which has brought us together today, without arms, without uniforms, without distinguished mark other than honorable scars, and in reviving and cherishing the memories and associations of the days that have passed we but strengthen that feeling of comradeship and brotherhood which makes stauncher friends more patriotic citizens, nobler men. This sentiment I would impress as an inspiration if not as a message from the new made tomb of a dead hero.

So ended the long and splendid life of "Old Swet." His dedication, resolve and courage were remarkable.

W. S. Featherston's grave in Hill Crest Cemetery.

Brig. Gen. Samuel Benton, C. S. A.
1820-1864

It was a scene that would be relived again and again in America's history, boys being sent off to war with community festivities at the train station. This time it was in Holly Springs, Mississippi, early Thursday morning, March 28, 1861. A large and enthusiastic crowd had gathered at the I. C. railroad station. With hostilities appearing imminent President Jefferson Davis had sent out the call throughout the South for volunteers and the young men of Marshall County answered with three full companies, The "Jeff Davis Rifles," "Home Guards," and the "Quitman Rifle Guards." How proudly they formed up, the rich, the poor, the notable, the unknown, the influential and the downtrodden, all with an invisible common bond, soldiers of the Confederacy. Mothers shed tears, fathers tried to hide the lumps in their throats, bands played and townsfolk wished them well as they prepared to depart from home, most for the first time ever and many of whom would never return. As part of the departure ceremonies, Miss Janie Edmonson, representing the delegation of young ladies from the Holly Springs Female Institute presented a beautiful hand sewn flag to the commander of the Jeff Davis Guards, Capt. Samuel Benton. Captain Benton received it on behalf of his men and stated; "The 25th of March, 1861, is a day to be remembered in the annals of Marshall County."

The people of Holly Springs felt good about their boys going off with forty year old Sam Benton, for he was highly respected. The nephew of Senator Thomas Hart Benton of Missouri, Sam Benton was born in Williamson County, Tennessee and had migrated to Holly Springs as a school teacher. He studied law, was admitted to the bar and became a prominent attorney as well as editor of The East Mississippi Times and state legislator in 1852. He was an "old line Whig" yet a strong believer in states rights and served as Marshall County's representative in the Secession Convention. His beautiful wife, the former Miss Knox of Holly Springs and their son, sadly waved good-bye as the train departed but must have also felt inward pride at Sam Benton's strong display of leadership.

The three companies boarded the train, proceeded to Corinth and joined with the "Corinth Rifles," "Lafayette Guards," " Horn Lake Volunteers," "The Invincibles," and "Panola Guards," to form the 9th Mississippi Infantry. By early 1862, Samuel Benton was elected colonel of the 37th Mississippi Infantry which was later reorganized as the 34th, including the "Tippah Rebels," "Dixie Guards," "Tippah Farmers," "Clarke County Rescuers," "Shubuta Guards," "Yancy Guards," and "McLemore Guards." Colonel Benton led them bravely at Shiloh, then assuming command of the 24th and 37th, he played a key role in the siege of Corinth. On to Perryville, Kentucky, where Benton was wounded, then at Murfreesboro and Tullahoma, Tennessee the Mississippians acquitted themselves well. By 1864, Colonel Benton found himself in command of an entire brigade when General Walthall was promoted to division command.

On July 22, 1864, Gen. Joseph E. Johnston's Corps was attempting to stop Gen. William Tecumseh Sherman's advance on the city of Atlanta. The bloody fighting which ensued that day resulted in over 3,700 Union and over 8,000 Confederate casualties, one of which was the dashing brigade commander, Samuel Benton. An artillery shell exploded just in front of Colonel Benton as he was leading his men in a charge toward the Union lines. A piece of searing shrapnel imbedded in his chest just above his heart and another jagged piece of metal tore away part of his right foot. They carried him to the rear and tried to stop the bleeding from the foot. In a makeshift hospital at Griffin, Georgia, the surgeons decided to amputate the right leg. Two days later, on July 28, 1864, not being able to recover from the massive loss of blood and the trauma caused by the wound in his chest and the loss of a leg, Samuel Benton died, far from the Holly Springs train station and his wife and son, and amidst the terrible suffering of his fellow Confederate soldiers. Back at his corps headquarters a telegram had just been transmitted containing the news that Col. Samuel Benton had been confirmed as brigadier general to rank from July 26, 1864, two days prior to his death. He was initially buried at Griffin, Georgia, near the field hospital where he died.

They Sleep Beneath the Mockingbird

Three years later a train pulled into the same Holly Springs railroad station where the boys departed in March, 1861, this time bearing the body of Samuel Benton. He had left as a captain and returned a fallen brigadier general to a solemn and grateful gathering and was buried with proper ceremony by his fellow veterans at Hill Crest Cemetery. A large monument was erected over his grave by the citizens of Holly Springs signifying a loving tribute to their fallen hero.

his beautiful head stone was erected over the final grave site where the body of General Benton was buried three years after his initial interment in Georgia.

Brig. Gen. Daniel Chevilette Govan, C. S. A.
1829-1911

He was twenty-one years old, single, college educated and adventurous when gold was struck in California in 1849. Unable to resist the temptation of the quest for untold riches D. C. Govan left Holly Springs, Mississippi, and joined his old friend Ben McCulloch who along with many other Mississippians and Tennesseeans were "westward-ho." Amidst the frantic chaos D. C. Govan and Ben McCulloch did not find the "mother lode" but McCulloch was elected sheriff of Sacramento and made Govan his deputy, leaving the gold fields for a much riskier life, attempting to maintain law and order among the forty-niners. Finally getting his fill of adventure he returned to picturesque Holly Springs, Mississippi in 1852, and settled in to the much calmer life of farming. He married the beautiful young daughter of Bishop James Harvey Otey of Tennessee, and the young couple finally settled in Phillips County, Arkansas, until the outbreak of the Civil War.

D. C. Govan raised a company and formed into the 2nd Arkansas Infantry and because of his law enforcement experience and his leadership abilities was elected colonel. They served in Cleburne's Division of Hardee's Corps and D. C. Govan led them gallantly in the great Battle of Shiloh, then at Perryville Kentucky. He had already earned command of a brigade in Cleburne's division by late 1862, and led them at Stone's River, Chickamauga, and Missionary Ridge and because of his conspicuous gallantry under fire was promoted to brigadier general to rank from February 29, 1863. General Joseph E. Johnston especially praised his conduct at the battle of Pickett's Mill on May 27, 1864.

During the Battle of Atlanta, General Govan and part of his brigade were overrun by Union soldiers after a vicious fight at Jonesboro. He and about six hundred of his men were captured by General Sherman's forces. Later paroled and exchanged he again led his men in the army of John Bell Hood and fought at Franklin and Nashville where on December 16, 1864, he was wounded in the throat and had to pass command. He recovered from the near fatal wound by March 18, 1865, when he again assumed command of his brigade and led them into North Carolina, and eventually to their final surrender.

When the war was finally over, D. C. Govan wanted nothing except to return to his farm on his Arkansas plantation in Marianna. He had been ruined financially but eventually recovered. In 1894, President Grover Cleveland appointed him Indian Agent, and he moved to Washington. Two years later, suffering the heavy loss inflicted by the death of his wife, he resigned and returned home, where he lived out the remainder of his life in Mississippi and Tennessee.

He was in Memphis, in the home of his daughter, Mrs. P. H. McKellar, 705 St. Paul Avenue when he died at 3 a.m on March 12, 1911. It was recorded on his death certificate that pulmonary edema was the cause of death, but perhaps the 84 year old general who had seen the fury of the gold rush, the blazing of cannon and clash of battle so many times, had lived through the perils of reconstruction and regained political notoriety, had a lovely family including several lovely children, had just lived himself out. He never discovered gold but he discovered Holly Springs, Mississippi, his boyhood home and the place where he often visited and sometimes resided after the war and a place that he chose to be buried. His funeral was conducted there at 10:30 a. m. on March 14, 1911. Burial followed in Hill Crest Cemetery with many confederate veterans at his graveside, comforting his grieving children, Mrs. P. H. McKellar, Mrs. J. J. Sample of Magnolia, Mississippi, and D. M. Govan, of Marianna, Arkansas. The body of the gallant general who was the son of Mary P. and Andrew Govan, a South Carolina congressman whose ancestors had fled Ireland to escape a bloody rebellion, was at last committed to the soil of the South in his beloved home of Holly Springs, Mississippi.

General Govan's headstone departs from the tall monuments so common in Hill Crest Cemetery. It lies flat and makes reference to his Arkansas regiment.

ST. PETERS CEMETERY
OXFORD

Brig. Gen. Claudius Wistar Sears

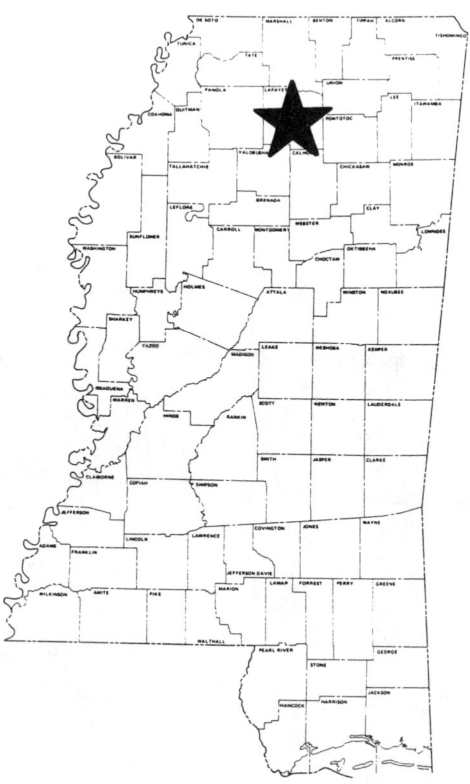

The world's great epics sing of men
That with the ages grow;
The classic deeds of heroes know
In history's afterglow.
When Fame makes up her honor roll
And writes, "For duty done,"
Man hath no brighter triumph gained
Nor greater guerdon won.

No less in war, where battling fronts
Flamed through the tragic day,
Than in the scenes of busy life,
Where peaceful arts held sway,
He was our patriot-hero still,
Whose life its message told,
And man shall write him honor-crowned,
And Fame his record hold.

Ossian D. Gorman

Located three blocks north of the town square, three blocks east on Jefferson, at the corner of Jefferson and North 16th streets.

Brig. Gen. Claudius Wistar Sears, C. S. A.
1817-1891

Each Sunday morning the silent pre-service meditation of the St. Peters Episcopal congregation of Oxford, Mississippi, would be softly interrupted by the rhythmic squeak of the cork leg straining under the weight of Gen. Claudius Sears as the bearded old man made his way down the isle to his vestry seat, unaware of the soft giggles of little children. The real leg had been left on the battlefield in Nashville on December 15, 1864, amputated after a ball passed cleanly through his horse "Billy" and wickedly tore through the tibia just below his left knee.

He was a brilliant man who became a renowned southern educator, mathematician and engineer. Although having been born in Massachusetts he so dearly loved the South that he spent his entire adult life there and often stated that if he could be born again it would be in Mississippi. Claudius Wistar Sears was a West Point graduate, class of 1841, with classmates William Tecumseh Sherman, W. S. Rosecrans, and James Longstreet. After serving in the Florida Indian Wars with the U. S. Army he resigned his commission to accept an offer from the Reverend Francis Hawkes, President of St. Thomas Hall in Holly Springs, Mississippi, to teach mathematics. He later followed Rev. Hawkes to Louisiana University (presently Tulane) and became its first professor of mathematics and physics. Sears returned to St. Thomas Hall in 1860 as president and taught there until the outbreak of war in 1861.

Claudius Sears joined company G, 17th Mississippi Regiment under the command of W. S. Featherston and was elected its captain. His unit was engaged at Manassas, Leesburg, and the five days battle around Richmond, and by December, 1862, he had risen to the rank of colonel of the 46th Mississippi Regiment. He fought Sherman at Chickasaw Bayou and was in the Battle of Port Gibson. He was present during the siege of Vicksburg, paroled and exchanged, and by early 1864, was serving under Gen. William Edwin Baldwin in Alabama when General Baldwin died from injuries received after falling from his horse. Sears assumed command of Baldwin's brigade composed of the 4th, 36th, 39th and 46th regiments and 7th battalion of Mississippi Infantry and was promoted to brigadier general to rank from March 1, 1864. He fearlessly led his brigade throughout the battle of Atlanta, Kennesaw Mountain, and throughout the Tennessee campaign participating in the battles of Franklin and Nashville.

It was during the battle of Nashville he received his only wound of the war, one which would end his days of soldiering. He was mounted upon his faithful horse "Billy" and was looking through his field glass to determine the position of the enemy when a shot passed through Billy and into Sears' left leg. One of his men, R. N. Rea of Brunette, Louisiana, wrote about the incident.

"...the ground was frozen hard and covered with deep snow..... everything was in confusion, and in the midst of all the sad surroundings and heartrending scenes of a fierce battle the grand old hero stood upon one foot, and with tears running down his cheeks, like a child, exclaimed: 'Poor Billy!, Poor Billy!' He did not seem to notice his own sad condition, but his whole attention and sympathy were directed toward the faithful steed which he had ridden during the entire war."

General Sears was carried to the rear in an ambulance wagon to the home of Mr. Ewing on the Franklin Pike. There, surgeon McCormick amputated his left leg just below the knee. Being too frail to travel with the army in their hasty retreat from Nashville he was left there as Generals Forrest and Walthall slowed the enemy down with aggressive rear guard actions. General Sears fell into enemy hands and was taken to the home of Dr. Burrill Abernathy, about 5 miles south of Pulaski where he was attended by Union surgeon Cooper. His old west point friend, Union Brig. Gen. George Henry Thomas, commander of his captors, extended him many personal courtesies and gave him parole. For Gen. Claudius Wistar Sears, the war was over.

Sears returned to Oxford, Mississippi and was elected to the Chair of Mathematics at the University of Mississippi, a position he held for twenty-five years while becoming one of the university's most noted professors and one of Oxford's most revered citizens. A devout church member, he was a member of the Vestry and a delegate to the Diocesan Council.

General Sears was paralyzed by a stroke on January 30, 1891, and died quietly in his home with his family near on Sunday, February 15, at 5:30 P.M. At his funeral in St. Peter's the next day, hundreds of mourners including many of the students and fellow veterans filled the church. He was interred in the beautiful St. Peters Cemetery, a few yards east of the grave of L. Q. C. Lamar.

General Sears' grave lies next to his wife in the southwest portion of the historic St. Peter's Cemetery, Oxford.

'DORO PLANTATION'
BOLIVAR COUNTY

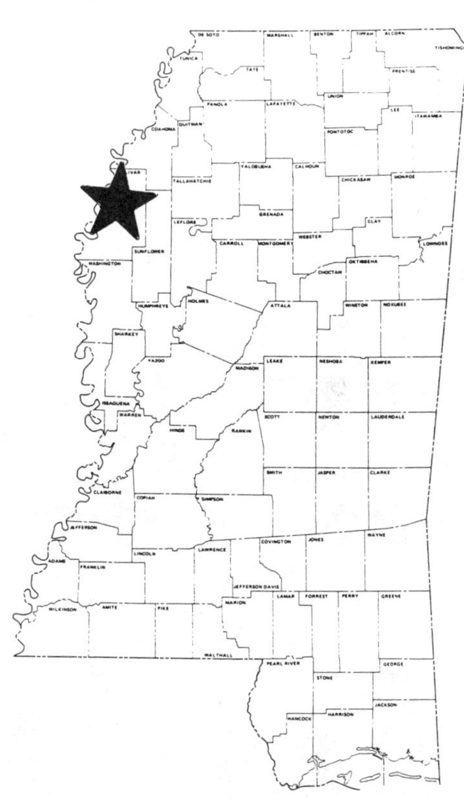

Brig. Gen. Charles Clark

O! Dixie land, fair Dixie land,
Thy memories linger with us yet;
We sing the glory of thy past-
We would not, if we could, forget.

O'er rocky crag and fertile field
War's fierce and cruel tide did sweep,
Now wild birds sing a requiem
In forest glades where heroes sleep.

As visions of the past arise,
Although the Southern star has set,
We listen to thy sacred lays-
We would not, if we could, forget.

The giant oaks still guard the hills
And crystal streams that once ran red,
The violets bloom among the vales
Sweet incense to our sainted dead.

We glory in our native land-
North, East, and West we love - and yet
The South is still our heritage-
We would not, if we could, forget.

The daises rear their graceful heads
On what was once a bloody plain,
Their snowy petals cover mounds
Where sweetly rest our noble slain.

Ah! dear old South, so staunch, so great!
We do not grieve, repine, regret,
But cherish thee within our hearts-
We would not, if we could, forget.

As nature's touch has healed the scars
Wrought deep by devastating hand,
So peace and love, the gifts of God,
Reveal a reunited land.

O, sunny land! our Dixie land,
Thy memories linger with us yet;
We love thee, honor - yea, adore-
We would not, if we could, forget.

Della Lamar West

Two miles south of Beulah on highway 1.

Brig. Gen. Charles Clark, C. S. A.
1811-1877

It was May 19, 1865, the great Civil War had ended a few weeks earlier. The chaotic uncertainty and apprehension in Mississippi bordered on panic. Hordes of deserters and stragglers along with homeless and confused freed slaves roamed the countryside. Criminals lurked everywhere, thousands of Confederate soldiers were returning, many permanently maimed, only to find in many cases their homes ransacked or burned, families scattered, livestock gone, and crops destroyed. The economy was in shambles, the agrarian lifestyle of subsistence without foundation.

The Governor of Mississippi was Brig. Gen. Charles Clark who was elected to succeed John J. Pettus in 1863. Governor Clark was in frail condition as he had been wounded in the shoulder at Shiloh and in the thigh at Baton Rouge so severely that he could stand only with aid of crutches. He was attempting to reestablish the government in Jackson. It had been "in transit" since the capture of Jackson by General Grant in 1863, first in Enterprise, then Meridian, Columbus and eventually Macon. Governor Clark convened the legislature in special session at the Capitol in Jackson on May 18. They became nervous when they received a report that breveted Union Gen. E. D. Osband, commanding federal forces at Jackson, had received orders from Washington to arrest each member if they attempted to convene. In a hurry, they passed a joint resolution, rules suspended, read three times and adopted, appointing three Commissioners to Washington to confer with President Johnson to learn what was necessary to bring the State back into the Union. Then they adjourned in great confusion and left town, the session lasting less than one hour.

At 7:30 a.m., the following morning, Governor Clark sat in the executive office of the State Capitol and was in conversation with his Attorney General, Judge T. J. Wharton and Col. J. D. Stewart. He was relieved to learn that Judge Wharton would accept the appointment as one of three Commissioners to Washington. Conversation suddenly ceased as the brisk footsteps of a platoon of Union soldiers could be heard coming down the hall, approaching the Governor's office. They were armed with rifles, bayonets fixed, and escorting General Osband. As they entered the doorway, General Osband politely saluted the Governor and read the following order:

"Sir, by orders received from superior headquarters based upon the instructions of the President of the United States, I am directed not to recognize the present civil Government of the State of Mississippi. Therefore as the representative of the Federal Government I must call upon you for the custody of the records and archives and Executive Mansion of the State of Mississippi to be held by me as public property until such time as legal representatives can be elected to take charge of the same. I desire to designate Monday the 22nd, May at 9 A.M. as the time and the State House as the place, when and where I will meet you with you to consummate this arrangement."

Governor Clark, slowly, and as best he could, raised himself from his chair, with great difficulty mounted his crutches, and standing as straight as his shattered hip would allow him defiantly said;

"General Osband, I denounce before high heaven and the civilized world this unparalleled act of tyranny and usurpation. I am the duly and Constitutionally elected Governor of the State of Mississippi, and would resist, if in my power, to the last extremity the enforcement of your order. I only yield obedience because I have no power to resist".

The Governor turned over the archives, mansion and executive authority to General Osband, returned to his Executive Residence in Macon, and there, two weeks later, he was arrested by Capt. Louis Keller, Co. A., 58th Ohio Volunteer Infantry under orders issued by Secretary of War Edwin M. Stanton and imprisoned at Fort Pulaski, Georgia, along with Governors Magrath of South Carolina and Allison of Florida.

They Sleep Beneath the Mockingbird

The personal diary of Capt. Keller, the arresting officer, contains the following entries:

"Was ordered to arrest Gov. Clark and report with him to Genl. Camby at New Orleans he is supposed to be at Macon, Miss. Got to Meridan (sic) at 5 p.m. stoped (sic) at the Jones Home the best in town but an awfull (sic) one the eating is horrible and bed likewise.

JUNE 6: Got to Macon at 11 a.m. Found the Gov. lived 1 mile from town found him at Home told him my unpleasant duty he communicated it to his Family every one of them got to crying it was a sorrowful night had to go out. Has a fine daughter. Missed the train sent the Gov. home till morning and had a good time with the 13th Ind. Cav. officers they are bricks as we call them in the Army. Went to see several Ladies some very pretty but all Reb.

JUNE 7: Had breakfast with Lt. Col Repper comdg. Post at Macon at 10. I went to Gov. and told him to get ready. He bid all his darkies good bye, go to Meredian (sic) at 3, had something to eat cost me $2. The Gov. had a bottle of Whiskey along took several drinks with him he is a jolly fellow can tell a few good jokes, he was a Brig. Gen. in Reb Army was crippled for life at the battle of Baton Rouge, and afterward elected Gov. of Miss. Got a good place for him to lie down in baggage car, after telling some yarns and taking a few drinks we lay down."

As Governor Clark lay in the baggage car of the slow moving train headed for prison, he no doubt considered the unusual chain of events that had brought him to his plight. He was born into a prominent Ohio family, one of ten children, and studied law in his youth. He was only in his early twenties when he and another law student took a sightseeing trip to New Orleans. As the steamboat docked in Natchez, young Charles and his friend disembarked for a look around. It was 1831, and Natchez was in its heyday. They were spellbound by the Spring fragrances and immense beauty of Natchez and as they walked down "lawyers row" they saw a sign on one of the buildings indicating that it was for sale. On the spur of the moment and with the irrepressible desire for adventure they inquired about the price. For a fifty dollar down payment it could be theirs on credit. They rushed back to the steamboat, borrowed the money from Clark's uncle, the captain of steamboat, and set up shop in Natchez. The next day the sign on the building read "Charles Clark and Cicero Jefferson, Attorneys"

Charles Clark prospered in Natchez. He taught school, passed the bar, and with the help of his newly found friends Gen. Thomas Hinds and Sgt. S. Prentiss he became popular enough to be elected to the State legislature in 1837, serving until 1844. Charles Clark moved to Fayette and married Eliza Darden of that city, one of the most beautiful girls from one of the most prominent families of that time.

He successfully tried a very famous case concerning property settlements with Indians with respect to the Treaty of Dancing Rabbit Creek and was paid his fee in land in the newly established Bolivar County where he later moved, helped clear and settle the "wild delta lands" and established a plantation called "Doro." (named from the chancery reference given the lawsuit John Doe V Richard Roe) At the outbreak of the Mexican War he organized an infantry company which became part of the 2nd Mississippi Infantry regiment and later became their colonel, succeeding Rueben Davis who became ill. Clark was present at the surrender of Santa Anna.

After the Mexican War, he returned to his plantation and by 1861, the 51 year old planter had amassed one of Mississippi's largest fortunes in land and slaves. When the State seceded from the Union Clark was one of the first to answer the call to arms organizing the "Bolivar Troop" The secession Convention appointed Clark, Van Dorn, Alcorn and Mott as brigadier generals of State troops with Jefferson Davis as major general. When Davis was called to the Presidency, Clark became Major General of State Troops but later relinquished that post for a brigadier generalship in the Confederate army.

General Clark was severely wounded in every major engagement in which he was involved. At Shiloh, in command of a division of troops under Albert Sydney Johnston, he was wounded in the shoulder on April 6, and had to relinquish command to be hospitalized. In the line of retreat at the Battle of Baton Rouge he received a wound to his thigh so severe that it was thought to be fatal and was left on the field to be captured by the enemy. As the Union surgeon was considering amputation of the leg, General Clark requested to be transferred to his friend in New Orleans, Dr. Stone. The surgeon concurred and Dr. Stone later reported on General Clark's critical condition:

"a fracture of the right thigh bone high up was aggravated by chronic disease of his right lung... should recover by the influence of a vigorous mind over a feeble frame."

His wife and children were allowed to pass through enemy lines to be with him during his convalescence.

Upon his exchange from captivity, General Clark, being physically unable to perform field duty, resigned from the Army in October, 1863, only to be elected Governor of Mississippi in November, receiving more than double the combined votes of his opponents, Rueben Davis and A. M. West. As Governor, General Clark presided over some of the darkest days of Mississippi's history as the War became more futile and victory impossible.

They Sleep Beneath the Mockingbird

So, as he rode in the discomfort of the baggage car toward his imprisonment at Fort Pulaski, the shattered body of General Clark unable to find rest certainly had much in common with the shattered dreams of the Confederacy and the State he loved so dearly. What would the future hold for them both? He had no way of knowing that he would be released within six months of his imprisonment by order of President Andrew Johnson, return to his beloved "Doro" and family, and there slowly reestablish his fortunes. His state would do likewise, after many dark years of reconstruction and military rule.

General Clark concluded his illustrious service to the State as a Chancery Judge of the fourth district, being appointed to that post by Governor Stone and making his circuit in a small buggy, driven by his grandson. He died on December 18, 1877, at "Doro" of pneumonia, the sixty six year old body finally yielding itself to the ages, and was buried in the family plot on an Indian mound near his house. In announcing his death Governor Stone referred to him as follows: "Eminent as a soldier, statesman and jurist, pure and guileless in private life, he has gone to his grave mourned by the People of the entire State."

Shortly after General Clark's release from federal prison, he was asked to address a joint session of the Legislature. He declined because of his status as a parolee but he wrote a letter urging re-unification and a speedy conservative course which would position Mississippi with equal political rights with her sister states in the Union. The letter also contained the following reference to the Union flag which exemplified his attitude of wisdom and courage:

"With one of you I marched under that flag in a foreign land, and it was victorious; with all of you I marched against it, and it was victorious; it again waves over us, is our flag, and may it ever be victorious."

But perhaps it was Judge T. J. Wharton who eulogized him best when he said:

"No one ever surpassed Charles Clark in the virtues and graces which adorned the position and which entitled the occupant of it to the lasting gratitude of his countrymen. He, like the immortal Quitman, and many others whose memories Mississippi will cherish with vestal fidelity was born outside the limits of what was called the 'slave holding states' but when the tocsin of war sounded and summoned to the field of deadly conflict the bravest and the best of the sons of both sections, he hurried to the standard of his adopted State and poured out his blood like water to hallow the cause which impelled Mississippi to attempt to sever the ties which bound her to the Union in defense of her honor and her Constitutional rights as a Sovereign State."

Governor Clark and his family lie on the crest of an old Indian Mound on the grounds of his plantation "Doro" in Bolivar County.

BRANDON CEMETERY
BRANDON

Brig. Gen. Robert Lowry

The silent flight of circling years
Has stilled the cannon's roar;
The echoing tramps of martial hosts
Fall on the ear no more;
The drums are stilled, the banners furled,
The dove of peace broods o'er our world.

To plowshares turned, the gleaming swords
Have stirred the trampled sod;
And where Death reaped his harvest dread
And souls went up to God,
Rich golden harvests meet our gaze,
The tall grass grows, and cattle graze.

The men and women who now fill
The many walks of life
Heard not the roar of hostile guns,
Saw not the deadly strife;
But parent lips have told the tale
How right 'gainst might could naught avail.

Though gallantly from town and farm
Thousands of patriots brave
Rushed hotly to the deadly fray
Their native land to save;
How bravely, daringly they fought,
And what heroic deeds they wrought.

And not alone through coming years
Shall human lips relate
Their noble deeds, but stone and bronze
Their fame perpetuate,
And moments of beauty prove
A grateful country's pride and love.

Be ours the task to keep alive
These memories sublime
By tongue and pen and sculptured stone
Throughout all coming time,
That men be stirred to emulate
The record of the good and great.

M. J. Haw

From Main Street in Brandon, turn north on College Street.

Brig. Gen. Robert Lowry, C. S. A.
1830-1910

Although Robert Lowry's last eighteen months on this earth were spent battling the long and painful illness of rheumatism, he always maintained a bright and cheerful spirit. He had been a hale and hearty man, a model for leadership in times of turmoil and a great patriarch of his State's efforts to regain its prominence so painfully stripped by the Civil War. He was one around whom thousands would rally for comfort and advice in those trying days and who had been most instrumental in overcoming the carpetbag rule of the post war years. He was a two term governor of Mississippi during some extremely difficult years (1881-1889), and afterwards resumed a lucrative law practice in Brandon and Jackson, but during his last months of waning health, his predominant memories must have been of the great battlefields of the war. In those final months he had time to draw from the vast repository of events stored in his memory from the proactive life lived in such a crucial time in our history.

It was 1861, in Rankin County where he answered the call to military service, enlisting in Company B, 6th Mississippi Infantry and being elected as major of that unit. In their subsequent combat engagement at Shiloh, Robert Lowry was wounded twice, once in the arm and once in the chest as his company lost three hundred and ten men out of their total number of four hundred and twenty five. They earned nicknames such as the "bloody sixth" and one historian described their ranks as "having been reduced to a burial squad." After his recuperation Lowry rejoined his regiment as their colonel in Corinth and led them into action in the battles of Second Corinth, Port Hudson, Port Gibson, Bayou Pierre, Champion Hill and Vicksburg.

They were the "Rankin Grays," "Rockport Steel Blades," "Lake Rebels," "Rankin Rough and Readys," and "Quitman Guards," and with Robert Lowry as their commander they were singled out many times for conspicuous gallantry. As part of the army of Gen. Joseph E. Johnston, Lowry's Mississippians fought bravely from Reseca to Atlanta and on into Gen. John Bell Hood's Tennessee campaign.

As they were heavily engaged in the bloody battle of Franklin, Tennessee, their Brigade commander, Gen. John Adams, was killed and Colonel Lowry immediately assumed command of the brigade, leading them fearlessly in one of the most intense battles of the war. Throughout the Battle of Nashville and the retreat from Tennessee the Mississippians fought fearlessly. Robert Lowry was promoted to brigadier general prior to their movements into North Carolina, to rank from February 4, 1865. General Lowry's Mississippians were engaged in the battle of Bentonville and later surrendered with Johnston in North Carolina. He was paroled in Greensboro in May, 1865, and with the remainder of his loyal brigade returned to his beloved home in Brandon, Mississippi and resumed his law practice with his colleague, Judge A. G. Mayers.

His thoughts of the terrible clash of armies and the din of battle came to a peaceful end at 9:30 Wednesday night, January 19, 1910 at the home of his granddaughter, Mrs. Webster E. Buie on State Street in Jackson. Although he had occupied offices that customarily were accompanied by great pomp and display, he was known to dislike such ceremony and because of this his family respectfully declined the offer of Governor Noel to allow his body to lie in state in the New State Capitol.

His funeral service was held at noon on Friday, January 21, 1910 at the W. M. Buie home. A special coach was added to the regular passenger train from Jackson to Brandon Friday afternoon to accommodate the body and the many legislators and other distinguished dignitaries who were to attend the interment in Brandon. Dr. C. F. Emory, pastor of the First Methodist Church assisted Dr. LaPrade, the officiating clergyman in conducting a very simple service at the grave site. After an eloquent prayer the members of the Robert A. Smith camp and the Rankin camp of Confederate Veterans, most of whom had served with the gallant commander, completed the burial in honor of their fallen comrade allowing no one else to use the shovels. Beautiful flowers were placed on the grave by the Brandon chapter of the Daughters of the Confederacy.

They Sleep Beneath the Mockingbird

Perhaps the official notice of Governor E. F. Noel to the Legislature on the day following the death of the gallant General and statesman best illustrates the loss so deeply felt by all Mississippians at the time of his death.

"The angel of death, last night called from life to eternity, one of Mississippi's noblest and most patriotic citizens, ex Governor Robert Lowry; A soldier without fear, a statesman without guile, and a gentleman above reproach has answered his last roll call. As Governor for eight years he gave to our State an efficient and honorable administration of public affairs. As an officer of the Confederacy and as commander of the Mississippi division of the United Confederate Veterans, he was true and tried, faithful to every duty and trusted and beloved by all with whom he was associated. Mississippians grieve at the departure of one whom they love to honor and extend to his family and friends their heartfelt sympathy. I desire to bring this sad intelligence officially to your notice that you may take such action as you may deem appropriate the occasion."

The Mississippi Legislature in turn issued the following resolution:

"Whereas, the Legislature has heard with profound sorrow of the death last night of the beloved and lamented Governor Robert Lowry, soldier, statesman and patriot who in war barred his breast to the bullets of the enemy, and in peace defended the rights of the people of his State with honor in himself and glory to her... therefore, be it resolved that the Legislature of the State of Mississippi do now in honor to his memory, adjourn to Monday, at 11:00 a.m. and attend his funeral in a body."

So came to an end the life of a man who braved many battles. Whether as a successful businessman, renowned attorney, effective legislator, brigadier general of Confederate infantry, Governor of Mississippi, notable historian who along with W. H. McCardle penned an illustrious history of Mississippi, or as the loving husband of Maria M. Gamage, and protective father of their eleven children, Gen. Robert L. Lowry always answered the call to duty and honor in service to the State he so dearly loved.

Governor Lowry and his wife lie beneath the tall monument pictured above in the Lowry family plot in the center of Brandon Cemetery.

'ARCOLE' FAMILY CEMETERY
WILKINSON COUNTY

Brig. Gen. William Lindsay Brandon

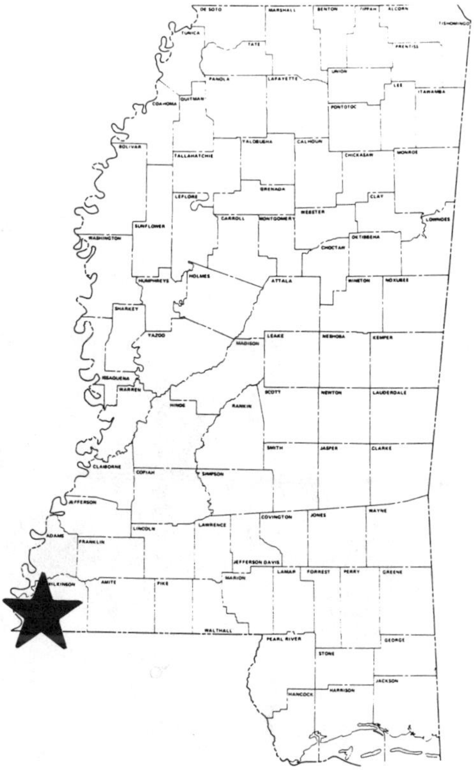

Come, cherished old comrade, your hand lay in mine!
We stood long ago on the fierce battle line;
No longer the fires of the bivouac gleam,
The scenes of the past are a vanishing dream;
The bugles are silent, the thrilling tattoo
Is beaten no more 'neath the hemlock and yew;
We fought on the mountain, we fought by the sea,
And now we both wait for the last reveille.

The hair that was dark is as white as the snow,
Our figures are bent and our footsteps are slow,
The rabbits are frisking to-day where we stood
With the foe in our front in the Georgian wood;
The wild, restless breezes are blowing the leaves
Where death cut his harvest and we were the sheaves;
And, sitting to-day 'neath the old crested tree,
We patiently wait for the last reveille.

Our battles we often live over again,
You with your crutches and I with my cane;
We think of the boys whom we left in the shade
Of hemlock and pine in some beautiful glade;
But, comrade so true, we will march nevermore,
Our battles are past and our triumphs are o'er;
In the twilight of life by the shores of the sea
We list for the sounds of the last reveille.

We followed the flag of the beautiful bars,
We bore it aloft through the smoke of the wars,
We cheered when its folds in their brilliancy shone
And victory's trophies came down to their own.
Our brave comrades sleep where the clear rivers run
Through patches of shadow and glimpses of sun;
They left us alone in the camps near the sea
To wait side by side for the last reveille.

The roses may bloom where we sleep in the spring,
Above us the robin her matins may sing,
For the river is flowing, its cadence is low,
And soon to the camps of our comrades we'll go;
But bring your chair closer, old comrade, that's right.
How closely we stood in the heat of the fight!
Though dim are our eyes, all the past we can see,
As we wait in our gray for the last reveille.

T. C. Harbaugh

Seventeen miles west of Woodville on the Pond-Peckneyville road and three and one-half miles west of Pond's store.

Brig. Gen. William Lindsay Brandon, C. S. A.
1800-1890

He was beginning the golden autumn of his life when the civil war began. A prominent planter with a fine plantation called "Arcole" which he had cleared from virgin forest just after Mississippi's statehood in a remote area south of historic Fort Adams, sixty year old William Lindsay Brandon had earned the admiration of all who knew him. He was the youngest of seven children His father, Gerard had narrowly escaped with his life from Ireland during a rebellion and came to the "new world" just in time to participate in the American Revolution serving with distinction in the Continental Army by defending Fort Moultrie and leading a cavalry charge at Kings Mountain. Gerard eventually settled in the Natchez district, then under Spanish rule, taking up land near old Washington. It was there around 1800 that future Confederate Gen. W. L. Brandon was born.

William Lindsay Brandon was educated in the finest schools. First in Virginia, then at Princeton, New Jersey, where he studied medicine. He returned to his home in Mississippi and established his plantation, "Arcole." Becoming interested in politics he helped his older brother, Gerard C., win the Governor's seat in 1827, then served in the Mississippi Legislature himself in 1835. He always had an affinity for military service, perhaps because of his father's reputation in the Revolution. He never passed up an opportunity to learn tactics and drill and eventually became major general of the district militia. In the Mexican War he served with distinction with Gen. Rueben Davis.

At the outbreak of the Civil War, William Lindsay Brandon was over 60 years old, had amassed a fortune from his plantation, owned over 300 slaves, and had three fine sons, Lane W., Robert L., and William R., who had been educated at Harvard, Yale, and Union College, New York, respectively. It would have been very understandable for him to stay on his plantation and supervise planting, but he immediately raised a company of volunteers, the "Jeff Davis Guards," and was elected their captain. His sons all enlisted as privates.

Then they were off to "Old Virginia" and mustered into service as Company D, Twenty-First regiment, Mississippi Volunteers, and placed under Longstreet's Corps, with W. L. Brandon as their colonel. In July, 1862, during the bloody engagement on the slopes of Malvern Hill during the Seven Day's Campaign, Colonel Brandon was hit above the foot by an artillery shell. He was taken to Richmond and his leg had to be amputated. It appeared to be life threatening. While in the hospital at Richmond, W. L. Brandon was visited by an old friend H. S. Van Eaton who expected to find him near death. Instead he found a cheerful and energetic old man clambering to find a way back into the war.

"I am doing first rate; I'll soon be out of this; my wound is doing well, healing by first intention, and in less than a month I'll be back with my regiment," replied Brandon. Mr. Van Eaton remarked; "I'm afraid, colonel, your fighting days are over." Colonel Brandon replied, "Not a bit of it; I'll live to give 'em fits yet."

He was indeed not finished. With the help of Dr. Redhead who fitted him with a wooden leg he joined his outfit in time for the Battle of Gettysburg where he assumed command of the 21st Mississippi regiment vice Benjamin Humphreys when Humphreys took over the brigade for General Barksdale who had fallen mortally wounded. On he fought at Chickamauga where his son, Capt. Lane Brandon was wounded. Then at Knoxville and back to Mississippi where after being promoted to brigadier general was placed in charge of Mississippi's bureau of Conscription.

When the war was over, General Brandon returned to "Arcole" where he lived out the remainder of his years. He was described by his son Robert as a man of marked character, who always loved humor and was fond of a good joke. He loved life, always kept packs of hunting dogs on his farm and invited his neighbors over frequently for hunts or dining, eschewed politics, was often called upon to settle disputes because of his trustworthiness and strong character, "was in height 6 feet

2 inches tall and weighed 200 pounds and until he was 86 years old would ride 16 miles to the county seat at Woodville and back sometimes the same day, always rode fine horses."

Gen. William Lindsay Brandon's long and rich life ended at 2 p.m. in his home at "Arcole" on October 8, 1890 at the age of 89. He was gently laid to rest just behind his home in the family plot with his family and friends in attendance. Today the gravesite has been overrun with growth, the plantation is abandoned and very little remains except the opulent and chivalrous history of one whose presence so brightly radiated with integrity, character, and intellect. Standing there you can almost sense his humor, vigor, and love of life in the surroundings he loved so dearly in a time and culture long since flown. A place where a hero lies buried, a hero who heard from his father the stories of the Revolution, who helped the pioneers tame the wilds of Mississippi, brandished cold steel in the swelters of Mexico, heard first hand the din of battle at Malvern Hill, Gettysburg, and Chickamauga, suffered the wicked torment of the amputation table, and who believed so firmly in the cause of southern independence that he offered up not only his full measure of service but that of his three sons to the field of battle. The fitting inscription on his headstone reads, "sans peur et sans reproche."

The burial site of General Brandon is located about one hundred yards behind his old home which is still standing at "Arcole." Time has not been kind to the burial ground of the general and his family, entangled and masked with new growth in random disarray, covering the order and beauty of the old, not unlike the fate of the "Old South."

CITY CEMETERY
NATCHEZ

Maj. Gen. William Thomas Martin
Brig. Gen. Thomas Pleasant Dockery
Brig. Gene. Zebulon York

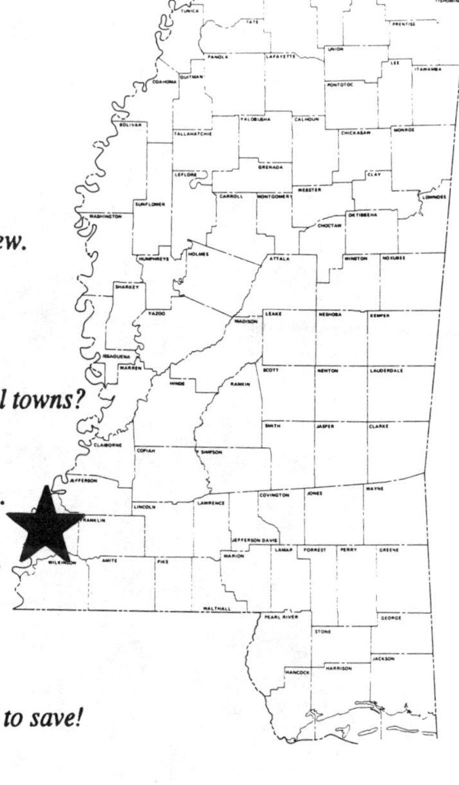

Remember the Bob White and Loblolly Pine,
Pristine pure water and mansions so fine?
Recall the white cotton and chivalry, too,
Walks through the garden in fresh morning dew.

River boats churning with wide paddle wheels,
Young colts at play in plush clover fields?
Women so lovely in fine gingham gowns,
Trains puffing steam plumes through beautiful towns?

Honor, respect, and love so sublime,
Fragrant peach orchards and muscadine vine.
Elegant ballrooms and children at play,
Families in church - so sincere did they pray.

Behold the great ruins of golden times past!
Of bountiful harvest, opportunity vast.
Oh weep for me not as you stand by my grave,
Just mourn for the Southland we fought hard to save!

H. A. Cross

Take business 61 to downtown Natchez, turn North on Canal Street, left on Madison, right on Lindenn to Cemetery Road.

Maj. Gen. William Thomas Martin, C. S. A
1823-1910

It was just after 5 p.m. when the funeral was concluded and the massive cortege was slowly proceeding from the Presbyterian Church to the City Cemetery in Natchez, Mississippi on the after-noon of Thursday, March 17, 1910. Masses of citizens were gathered on both sides of the road along the way, flags on boats in the port, above the Chamber of Commerce, and the Post Office were flying at half mast - businesses closed. As the procession passed the commons on which a boys baseball game was underway, the youths stopped play, and placed their caps over their hearts in final tribute to an eighty seven year old former Civil War general of Cavalry, Maj. Gen. William Thomas Martin.

Most of the young boys were more familiar with General Martin as the Natchez postmaster appointed by President Teddy Roosevelt, a job that he had recently given up due to his failing health. Some may have remembered him as an appointee to the State Flag Commission which selected the present design of Mississippi's colors containing the Confederate stars and bars; or as a delegate to the Mississippi's 1890 Constitutional Convention, who after being a major architect of its design, refused to sign it because of reservations with section 258. Some would have heard their fathers speak of him as a State Senator from 1882-1894, a trustee of the University of Mississippi and Jefferson College, the president of the Natchez, Jackson, and Columbus Railroad, or as a duly elected Congressman from Mississippi in 1868, who was denied his rightful seat in Washington. And maybe some recalled his love of history in his position as vice president of the Mississippi Historical Society. But they were all too young, much too young, to focus on his most daring exploits, those of a dashing and intrepid major general of Cavalry of the Confederate States Army.

He was not a native Natchezian, having been born in Glasgow, Kentucky on March 25, 1823. After graduation from Centre College (now Central University) at age 17, he moved to Vicksburg with his family and studied law in the office of his father, John Henderson. He was admitted to the bar in 1844, and married Margaret Dunlop Conner of Natchez. Martin was elected district attorney of the 1st Judicial District, was a Whig in politics and against secession, but after the Mississippi seceded he offered his services, enlisting in the "Adams Troop" when it was organized in May, 1861. His popularity and strong character was responsible for him being elected as their captain. They deployed to Virginia for training and in Richmond and became part of the 2nd Mississippi Cavalry and attached to the Jeff Davis Legion with Martin elevated to the rank of major.

They arrived at Manassas one day after the battle there, but were later engaged at Falls Church, Virginia, Martin's cavalry receiving favorable mention from Generals G.W. Smith and Joseph E. Johnston. He led his brave cavalry throughout the siege of Yorktown and the battle of Williamsburg where he was wounded. Martin was promoted to lieutenant.colonel just before the Seven Days Battle around Richmond and was commanding the Jeff Davis Legion. He accompanied J.E.B. Stuart in his daring and famous ride around McClellan in the Peninsula Campaign along with Colonels Fitzhugh Lee and W.H.F. Lee, capturing many prisoners and critical supplies, and was promoted to brigadier general of Cavalry on December 2, 1862.

His cavalry thundered on into Tennessee in 1863 as General Martin was placed in command of a division consisting of Roddey's and Cosby's brigades. He was with Gen. Earl Van Dorn in his Spring Hill, Tennessee victory, then accompanied Gen. James Longstreet into East Tennessee. By November 10, 1863, he had earned the commission of major general of Cavalry and continued with Wheeler's corps at Shelbyville, Tullahoma, Chickamauga, Clinch River, Maryville, Siege of Knoxville, Fair Garden, and Mossy Creek, then with Generals Johnston and Hood from Dalton to the Fall of Atlanta. After a dispute with General Wheeler he left for his final assignment in command of the district of Northwest Mississippi. He surrendered with Dick Taylor's command in May, 1865.

His accomplishments after the war, as previously mentioned, were impressive.

He survived the perils and dangers of combat to give much more of his talents and energies to his fellow man in a time when they were most needed.

Gen. William Thomas Martin lived to age gracefully after a long and productive life. On March 10, 1910, he was in his library at his beautiful mansion "Monteigne" on the outskirts of Natchez when he suffered a stroke of apoplexy. He fell to the floor striking his head resulting in a severe concussion. He lingered for about a week coming in and out of consciousness, then with his family at his side he quietly died at 5:40 p.m. on Wednesday, March 16, in his bedroom at "Monteigne" in his eighty-eighth year. According to his prior wishes they dressed him in his uniform he wore as a major general of Cavalry and placed him in a casket draped with a Confederate flag. The pall bearers were his sons and son-in-law, Lewis R. Martin, cashier of the Bank of Commerce, Farrar Martin, vice-president of the Britton and Koontz Bank, Judge William C. Martin, City Solicitor, John H. Martin of Baird Shields in Natchez, and W. R. Luckett of Vicksburg. Honorary pall bearers were Major Douglas Walworth, Major Richard E. Conner, J. C. Carson, Volney D. Fowler, Judge Wade R. Young, Dr. Bisland Shields, and J. P. Green.

By the time the graveside ceremonies were concluded, the baseball game had finished. But the young men must have heard the volleys fired at the graveside by the rifle squad from Company C, Third Regiment of the Mississippi National Guard consisting of privates Charles Darden, Joseph Dixon, Willis McDonald, and Tucker Gibson. They probably heard the taps blown by Professor William Ennis at sunset as they concluded their game. And they probably sensed that this funeral was not ordinary, that a hero had just been buried, which might have explained the unusual sight of tears they saw running down the cheeks of the old Confederate Veterans who were marching behind the coffin.

General Martin's lovely monument in Natchez City Cemetery anchors the family plot in the midst of one of Mississippi's most historic burial grounds.

Brig. Gen. Thomas Pleasant Dockery, C. S. A.
1833-1898

A beautiful woman in her late twenties came to call on General Ulysses S. Grant at his headquarters near Vicksburg on July 3, 1863. She was Octavia West Dockery of Claiborne County, the daughter of ex-Governor Cato West of the Mississippi Territory and wife of General Thomas Pleasant Dockery of Arkansas, one of Major General John Bowen's commanders holding out in desperation inside the City of Vicksburg. She was frantic to learn of her husband's fate since rumors of starvation, sickness and death ran rampant and she and her young children had heard nothing from him for weeks. General Grant cordially received Mrs. Dockery and listened with great understanding and sympathy as she fervently requested permission to enter the city and inquire of the well being of her husband. He informed her that he could not violate his own order" to permit no one to enter until all the details of the surrender were completed". But in an unusual act of kindness he sent one of his orderlies directly to General Pemberton to inquire about General Dockery while Mrs. Dockery waited at his headquarters for the news. According to witnesses, "the scene between General Grant and Mrs. Dockery was a very touching one when the orderly returned and General Pemberton informed General Grant that General Dockery was uninjured and in good health, and would visit Mrs. Dockery as soon as General Grant would permit." That reunion took place shortly since the final details of surrender included parole for the officers and men.

Thomas Pleasant Dockery was no stranger to hardship and deprivation and would certainly ask no favor for himself that was not afforded to his men As one of his men once noted, "he never said 'go on', but 'come on' into the thickest of battle". He was born into a family of revolutionary ancestry in North Carolina on December 18, 1833. His father, Captain John Dockery relocated to Columbia County in southern Arkansas when Tom was nineteen and established a large plantation called "Lamartine". It was there that Thomas Pleasant Dockery became one of the most prominent Arkansans as he and his father pioneered the Methodist Church and the Masonic Lodge. The young Tom Dockery became a highly educated, fluent speaker, and trusted State legislator, and by the time of the outbreak of the War was one of the most prominent and hospitable men of the area and had married well, to the beautiful Octavia West of Mississippi.

In early 1861, Tom Dockery organized and personally equipped a local regiment, the 5th Arkansas, later mustered into the nineteenth Arkansas infantry of which he became colonel. They saw their first action as state troops at the Battle of Wilson's Creek under General Ben McCulloch, where they were credited with outflanking the federal troops and leading the final victorious charge. With Major General Earl Van Dorn and as regular confederate army troops they fought in the Battle of Corinth in May, 1862, then with Sterling Price came back to Arkansas to temporarily command the middle subdistrict of Arkansas. Tom Dockery was back with his old regiment as commander of the 2nd brigade of General John S. Bowen's Division in the battles leading up to and including the siege of Vicksburg where General Stephen Dill Lee lauded Dockery for his coolness and bravery.

Thomas Pleasant Dockery rejoined his lovely wife and precious daughters after the siege of Vicksburg, but only for a short while. After his exchange he was promoted to brigadier general to rank from August 10, 1863, and again led his brigade of Arkansans in the 1864 Camden Expedition at Mark's Mills and Jenkin's Ferry, fighting with conspicuous bravery.

After the surrender of his troops in 1865, Dockery returned to Arkansas only to find out that his wealth had been wiped away by the war. He nevertheless continued to serve with distinction. According to his obituary; "he served faithfully and with distinction during the war, and when all the swords were sheathed he took a leading part in the councils of his State and did much towards allaying the rigors of the reconstruction period."

Another newspaper reported; "..in the year when Arkansas was the scene of bloodshed in a political war, General Dockery was called upon by the Democratic governor to defend him against armed Republicans who were in possession of the statehouse. He was made military governor to command. One of the hottest and bloodiest of State wars ensued. General Dockery at the head of State troops reinstated Baxter, Democratic Governor, in the statehouse."

Tom Dockery later took up the profession of civil engineering and removed to Houston, Texas where he found work with the city, eventually becoming fiscal agent for Houston, with his office located in the financial hub of New York City. His two daughters, Nydia Dockery (Mrs. R. H. Foreman) and Miss Octavia Dockery, named after her deceased mother, returned south to Natchez.

On February 26, 1898, General Thomas Pleasant Dockery died unexpectedly in New York City, far away from the southland he fought so bravely to protect. His death certificate listed the cause as rheumatiod endocarditis and pulmonary edema. At the request of his daughters his body was shipped by train to Natchez for burial. The casket bearing General Dockery's remains arrived in Natchez on Friday evening, March 4, over the New Orleans and Northwestern Railway. The burial was conducted on March 5, at Natchez City Cemetery, with the Reverend T. B. Holloman, pastor of the Jefferson Street Methodist Church and the Reverend Dr. W. H. Neel pastor of the Presbyterian Church presiding. According to his obituary notice;

"the casket was uncovered in order that the face might be viewed for the last time by the mourning relatives and friends of the deceased. The features were almost perfectly preserved, and had more the appearance of one reprising in a sweet and gentle slumber than one in the embrace of the long and eternal sleep that knows no waking. This was a source of great consolation to those who stood round the bier and aided in assuaging the deep and poignant grief felt by all."

General Thomas Pleasant Dockery was peacefully interred in the surroundings very near the battle sites where he had seen so much violence in the Civil War, and not far south of Vicksburg where he poured out his full measure of resistance in 1863. At his gravesite stands a marker erected by members of the United Confederate Veterans Organization. A wreath with the inscription "Arkansas", recently place there by a contingent of Arkansans, stands as a silent yet perpetual "thank you" to the general who "bore the battle".

General Dockery's grave lies peacefully in Natchez Cemetery next to his daughter, Octavia, decorated with a Southern Cross of Honor and an Arkansas memorial wreath.

Brig. Gen. Zebulon York, C. S. A.
1819-1900

On the front porch of the York House, a Natchez, Mississippi boarding house near the turn of the century, an old man with an empty left sleeve could often be seen slowly rocking and gazing stoically westward toward Louisiana, probably reminiscing on his lost fortunes. He was Zeb York, the proprietor of the York House and one who had once reaped the full benefits of the "Old South".

Born in Avon, Maine, on October 10, 1819, Zebulon York's roots ran deep in American history. He was the son of an officer in the War of 1812, the grandson of a warrior who fought with distinction in the American Revolution.His maternal grandfather was present at the surrender of Cornwallis. Zeb York was afforded a strong education from his early youth, first at Wesleyan Seminary in Kent's Hill Maine, then graduating with honors from Transylvannia University in Kentucky at the age of 16. In his further quest for education he came south and attended Louisiana University (Tulane) to study law and there fell in love with the South. Upon graduation he decided to make it his permanent home and began law practice in Vidalia, Louisiana, in the firm of Stacey & Sparrow. His strong intellect and diverse travels helped York to soon become the leading attorney of that Parish. It was there that he slowly became ingrained in the plantation lifesyle, plowing his lucrative law earnings into parcels of land for planting. By 1861, Zebulon York owned six magnificent plantations and over 1,700 slaves, many thousand head of livestock, and produced 4,500 bales of cotton each year. He was a multi-millionaire, the "beau ideal" of Southern aristocracy, and by the time the Civil War broke out, York and his partner, Mr. Hoover, had the distinct honor of being Louisiana's largest taxpayers.

In addition to his strong philosophical commitment to the Southern cause, the outcome of hostilities between the North and South meant quite a lot to Zebulon York financially. He wasted no time in forming an artillery company which along with a local infantry company constituted the 14th Louisiana Infantry with York as its major. They went north, to Virginia, to train and fight. Soon, having been promoted to lieutenant colonel and assigned to General John Magruder's division, York and his Louisianans were instrumental in the success of his Peninsula Campaign, completely deceiving General Mclellan as to the size of their force and causing his withdrawal form Yorktown. Later at the Battle of Williamsburg, York was wounded in three places from one bullet. After recuperation, and now a full colonel in command of the regiment, he fought bravely at Mechanicsville, Frazer's Farm and Malvern Hill. On August 29, 1862, while attempting to capture a railroad line at the Battle of Second Manassas he was severely wounded in the neck and had to be given a furlough.

York came home to Louisiana for rest and recuperation but while on furlough Union intelligence learned of his whereabouts and an attempt was made at his capture. He managed to barely escape his captors and returned to his unit in time to participate in Gettysburg and the Battle of the Wilderness. Zeb York was promoted to the rank of brigadier general to rank from May 31, 1864. Then, during the third battle of Winchester in the Shenandoah Valley on September 19, 1864, General York's left arm was shattered by a cannon shell. It fell useless and although being dressed and nurtured it later required amputation as the result of severe pain, infection, and incapacity. Although unable to meet physical demands of command in the field, General York assisted in recruiting foreign-born prisoners of war for Confederate service and at the end of the war led a small group of soldiers at Yodkin's bridge providing security for President Davis and his cabinet in their flight from Richmond.

The war ended with Zebulon York financially ruined. His slaves were freed, his livestock long since confiscated, his plantations in ruins and unable to produce, and his debts mounting. He eventually left it all and settled in Natchez where after several years of hard work he became proprietor of the York House and spent his aging days conversant with boarders comparing stories about the war. No doubt he often contemplated what might have been if the South had been the victor, if the fickle winds of fate had blown just slightly in the other direction.

The end came as the result of a stroke on Sunday afternoon, August 5, 1900. The funeral was held on the morning of Tuesday, August 7, at St. Mary's Cathedral. It was largely attended as he had gained the love and respect of his adopted Natchezians. They proceeded to the City Cemetery and laid him to rest amidst beautiful floral decor. He was survived only by his wife. He lies today in a lovely fenced plot with a headstone which reads "erected by veterans".

In death it was his fellow veterans who best understood the sacrifices of one whose lineage reached so deeply into our nation's beginnings; who left a secure foundation in the North to seek fortunes in the South and, after leaving an arm in Virginia in service to the cause he held so dear, returned, though impoverished, to live out his final years and take his eternal rest in her fertile soil.

The somewhat weathered monument over the grave of Zeb York in the Natchez City Cemetery was placed there by his fellow veterans shortly after his death.

OLD GREENSBORO CEMETERY
TOMNOLEN, WEBSTER COUNTY

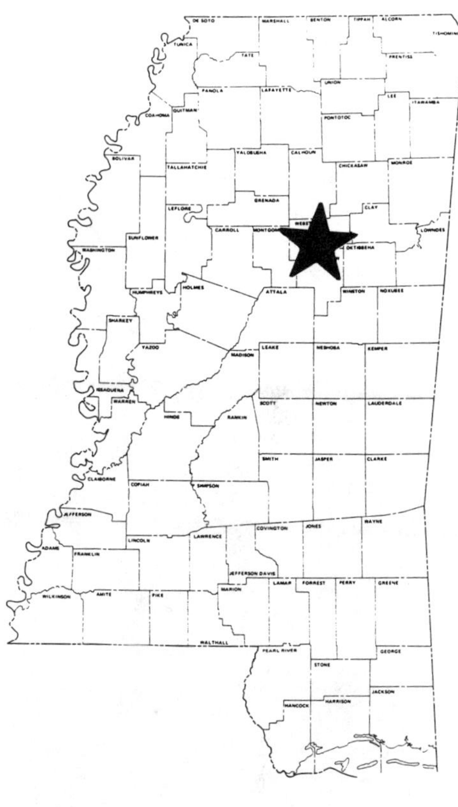

Brigadier General William Felix Brantley

Out of the years that long ago vanished
Back from a youth that has flitted doth come,
Mingled with laughter and burdened with sorrow,
The stirring tattoo of an old army drum;
And dimly I see where a river is flowing
The glimmer of lights, forming long, ghastly lines,
And and army in gray amid silence is marching
Under the crest of the far-away pines.

Hark? 'twas a bugle; I certainly heard it,
'twas a call for a charge through the copse on the foe,
And yonder a flag in the starlight is waving
The blessed old bars of the long, long ago;
The legions of gray in the valley are forming,
The guns are at work on the crest of the hill,
A comrade goes down with a prayer for his mother;
The roar of the fight not a moment is still.

Nay, 'tis but a dream of the days that are over;
The crutch at my side is a token, I say,
Of a youth that was splendid, a boyhood enhallowed,
When proudly I sported a jacket of gray,
When shoulder to shoulder we marched on to glory
And charged in our youth to the cannon's red mouth,
When victory perched on our beautiful banner
And fame wove a wreath for the chivalrous South.

There's gray in my hair as I sit in the gloaming;
'Twas gold when we stood on the battle lines,
And I think of the lock that I sent to a sweetheart
Who waited for me in the shade of the pines.
And so by the brink of the mystical river
That wanders away to the uttermost sea
I dream of my comrades of march and of battle,
I dream of the beautiful banner of Lee.

We furled it, the ages will crown it with glory;
We lost, but the halo of fame is our own-
No stain on the swords that we drew for the Southland,
And not a regret where our bayonets shone.
I hear a sweet voice that is constantly calling
With love in its tones from a land far away,
And I yearn as I sit in the mystical shadows
For the heavenly camp of the comrades of gray;

T. C. Harbaugh

Located eight miles west of Eupora on highway 82, then north at "old Greensboro" historical marker.

Brig. Gen. William Felix Brantley, C. S. A.
1830-1870

November 2, 1870 was a clear day in Winona, Mississippi, a good day to travel. The thick summer foliage had given way to the first bite of fall but was yet thick enough along the roadside to conceal stealthy assassins poised in their cowardly surveillance awaiting their unsuspecting prey. Their target was General William Brantley who had just left Winona on his way to his home near Old Greensboro. It was approaching 9 o'clock in the morning and the thirty nine year old General had plenty of time to make the twenty mile journey riding in his buggy accompanied by a black youth and more than likely keeping countenance with his many memories of the Civil War as well as his current legal case load.

There had been trouble, and that was the purpose for General Brantley's visit to Winona. Dr. Arnold Brantley, the Mayor of Winona, and the general's brother had recently been shot and killed while attending a church concert and another relative, Captain Conner, a member of the Mississippi Legislature, was also murdered a short time later. General Brantley vowed to find the murderers and even though being warned of possible danger to himself he did not relent. It had been a long standing feud which, starting in Texas long before the war, maturing into violence between the Brantleys and the Bolzells, and had claimed several other victims. A friend cautioned the General about travelling predicted routes whereupon he characteristically responded, "Whenever it is so that I cannot go wherever business calls me, then I want them to kill me."

He was about a half mile East of Winona when the calm November morning suddenly exploded with multiple shotgun blasts from the hidden shooters. The general did not have time to react in defense. His body was riddled with at least twenty-five buckshot and he died instantly, his passenger was unhurt. Witnesses from town heard the shots and saw smoke from the brush along the roadside. Tracks were followed to a nearby marsh but the perpetrators were not apprehended and their identity never known.

The violent act had robbed the State of one of her true heroes and the South one of her bravest leaders. History had somewhat harshly judged him, probably because of his sometimes firm and focused personality. He was a stern disciplinarian of his troops. As one historian described him;

"he was a man who had a broad mental grasp, coupled with great personal courage, and the unyielding tenacity of purpose, which from the start brought him success to his chosen profession, and which assured him fame and fortune".

William Brantley was a delegate to Mississippi's secession convention, and after the call to arms he helped organize the Wigfall Rifles, a local company which elected Brantley as their Captain. The Wigfall Rifles trained at Camp Clark near Corinth and were later mustered into the 15th Mississippi Infantry regiment as Company D. Later as commander of the 15th Mississippi Regiment, Major Brantley let his troops into the battle at Shiloh where he was severely wounded in fighting near the Peach Orchard. After recovering from his wound and as Colonel of the 29th Mississippi Regiment he distinguished himself in the battle of Murphreesboro and Stone's River where he was again wounded, captured, and through self discipline and cunning, made a quick, daring escape from his enemy to resume the command of his troops. He continued in all the battles in which the Army of the Tennessee was engaged including Chickamauga, and Atlanta. He was promoted to Brigadier General on July 26, 1864 after his brigade commander, General Benton was mortally wounded near Atlanta. He continued with distinction throughout the war and surrendered the remnants of his brigade at Greensboro, North Carolina in April, 1865. Major General Edward Cary Walthall gave note to his "skill, activity, zeal, and courage", and Lieutenant General Stephen Dill Lee, his corps commander said in referring to Brantley's action against the Chattanooga and Atlanta railroad, the investment of Resaca and the holding of Snake Creek Gap against Sherman's Army;

They Sleep Beneath the Mockingbird

"The brigades of Sharp and Brantley particularly distinguished themselves.... Brantley was exposed to a severe efilade fire. These noble brigades never faltered in this terrible night struggle... I have never seen greater evidences of gallantry that was displayed by this division."

Joining with John Bell Hood's Army in Northern Alabama, General Brantley took part in the bloody actions into Tennessee including Franklin where his unit suffered heavy casualties. He joined Joseph E. Johnston's effort into North Carolina and there surrendered with Johnston on April 26, 1865, having only 183 effectives remaining in his brigade.

In an obituary, the Semi-Weekly Clarion of Jackson referred to General Brantley as follows:

"He was one who was never known to pale or waver before any foe in private life or on the field of battle — but for whom it was reserved to fall by cowardly and brutal assassination."

General William Felix Brantley was laid to rest behind the church at Old Greensboro, on November 3, 1870. He left a wife, and a little girl, a sister and brother. An impressive monument engraved with his likeness was later erected at his gravesite to perpetuate his memory and to honor his long and untiring service.

The assasins were never found. The mystery of his death remains forever encased in the passage of time.A striking monument stands over the grave

A striking monument stands over the grave of General Brantley in the cemetery behind Old Greensboro Church, complete with a bust of the general made from his death mask. Part of the ear is missing from the buckshot of the assassins.

ROBINETTE CEMETERY
CORINTH

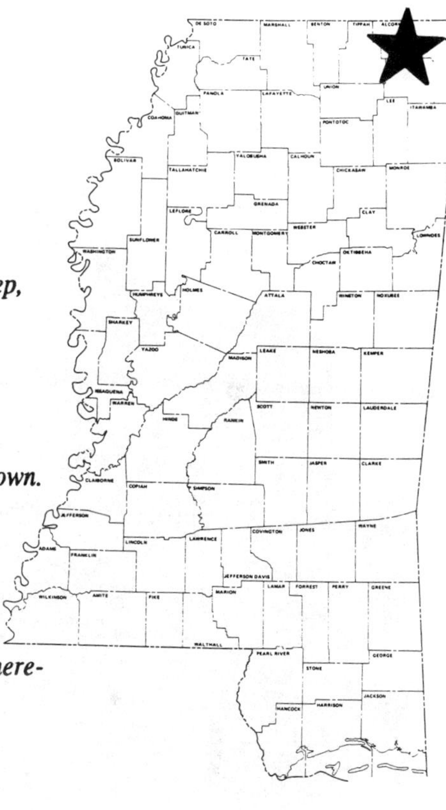

Brigadier General Joseph Lewis Hogg

Furled are the banners, our heroes are dead;
Faded the echoes that followed their tread.
Hushed is the music that wakened their day;
Silent the dirges that bore them away.

All through the Southland we've laid them to sleep,
Buried our loved ones adown in the deep.
Some on the summit of mountain and hill;
Some in the valleys, all peaceful and still.

Others are lying with loved ones at home;
Thousands we weep for whose graves are unknown.
Sacred the twilight that shroudeth each stone;
Mothers have knelt there and sorrowed alone.

Ave Marias and prayers have been said;
Crushed and forsaken, our tears we have shed.
Lay down your garlands, Place laurel wreaths there-
Purest of flowers and all that is fair.

Cherish forever their resting place green;
Weep in your hearts for the army unseen.
Sing, O ye poets, of soldiers in gray;
Monuments raise ye above their old clay.

Hushed are the cannon; they faced them nor fled.
Peacefully sleep ye, Confederate dead.
Louise Cary Page

From highway 72 turn north on State Street, left on Fulton Drive, then left on Linden Street. (Battery Robinette)

Brig. Gen. Joseph Lewis Hogg, C. S. A.
1806-1862

The crowded troop train approached Corinth, Mississippi, in April, 1862 from Memphis nearing its top speed of 30 miles per hour and carrying a brigade of Texas troops augmented with an Arkansas battalion, all commanded by Brigadier General Joseph Lewis Hogg of Texas. It had been a long trip and they were late- too late for their intended purpose of helping at Shiloh since General Beauregard's troops had just fallen back into Corinth after the bloody battle. Their delay was primarily caused by the necessity of boarding a steamer up the river to Memphis from Duvall's Bluff after dismounting and sending their horses home. Then there was some delay in requisitioning the needed supplies in Memphis.

It was too crowded to enter Corinth with over a thousand new men, so the train carrying the Texans stopped about two miles west of town where General Hogg and his brigade disembarked and set up camp. They became part of General Beauregard's Army and immediately began to prepare for the defense of Corinth from certain attack by Union General Halleck's forces pursuing from Shiloh.

From the beginning of hostilities between the North and South in 1861, the strategic importance of the little town of Corinth in extreme northeast Mississippi was apparent to military planners of both sides. It was there that the Memphis and Charleston railroad intersected the newly completed Mobile and Ohio creating a pathway to the entire South. The small village of Cross City which sprang up there seven years earlier and later renamed Corinth had, by the time of the War, grown to a population of 1,200.

Masses of newly recruited Confederate troops began to flow into Corinth from every direction for mobilization, training, and further assignments in Mobile, Pensacola, Virginia, and Kentucky. By the spring of 1862, just prior to the Battle of Shiloh, over sixty thousand men were concentrated around Corinth. Men from all over the South, most of whom had never been more than twenty miles from their homes were crowded into close encampments, their immune systems not having adjusted, the food and water sources beomining polluted from the high concentration of men and animals, while hygiene and medical facilities were in a terribly crude state. The results was sickness on a mass scale.

Many more died of sickness than from battle and perhaps the most cruel form of sickness was dysentery, an inflammatory disease of the bowel. It usually began by severely dehydrating the body with diarrhea, then inflamming the colon resulting in profuse bleeding. Bacteria would enter the abdominal cavity causing massive infection. Strong physical constitutions would be rendered weak and frail, high spirits shattered, and in most cases, death followed slowly and painfully. Dysentery, sometimes referred to in those days as "the flux" was no respector of rank, status, or wealth, and tragically it was the malady of youthful, high spirited, newly commissioned Brigadier General Joseph Lewis Hogg. General Hogg was taken ill only a few days after the arrival of his brigade in Corinth.

Because of the tremendous strain on medical facilities in and around Corinth in the aftermath of Shiloh, General Hogg was taken to a private residence about four miles west of town and there was attended by his brigade surgeon Dr. Wallace McDugald and his faithful servant Bob who was constantly at his side throughout his illness. Dr. McDugald used everything at his disposal but with the limited knowledge of the disease at the time, General Hogg's condition worsened. His oldest son, Thomas Hogg, a private in Company C, 3rd Texas Cavalry of Hogg's brigade was summonsed to his bedside when his condition became critical. Throughout the pain and suffering of the dread disease General Hogg's main concern was his absence from his men at a time when heavy skirmishing was beginning north of Corinth as General Halleck's troops approached. According to his son, the inability of the General to lead his men in this action hastened his death.

General Joseph Lewis Hogg's emaciated body finally succumbed to the "flux" on May 16, 1862, as fighting raged around Farmington. He was buried near Mount

Holly School House with a brief service conducted by his staff and men.In 1918, General Hogg's partial remains were disinterred and placed under a monument which was erected by the State of Texas at Fort Robinette in Corinth.

He died without having seen a battle in the Great Civil War and so quickly that he had not the opportunity to don the full regalia of a Confederate general, but he knew war well. He had served with his home state of Texas in the Mexican War in 1846, as a private, and was conspicuous for gallantry. He commanded a regiment of troops in the Alabama militia as a young colonel when he was a planter in the Tuscaloosa area prior to moving to Texas. He was Major General of Texas troops prior to the war.

The statesmanship of Joseph Lewis Hogg was equally notable. As a member of Congress of the Republic of Texas in 1843, he championed the cause of annexation and was a member of Texas' first Constitutional Convention. He later served in the Texas Senate as chairman of the Judiciary Committee, and was a pioneer promoter of railroad development of that state. His son James Stephen Hogg became the first native governor of Texas. Joe Hogg was a member of the Texas Secession Convention and was among the first to raise troops for service in the Confederacy.

The dread disease of dysentery unfairly cut short the promising career of one of Texas most dedicated and focused leaders far from his home of Rusk, Texas, but the partial remains of the son of Thomas Hogg, a colonel in the Revolutionary War and the grandson of John Hogg, an early Irish immigrant to the new colony of Virginia, lie honorably and peacefully under the beautiful monument that bears his name within the hallowed breastworks of Fort Robinette very near where he disembarked his men in the early days of this nation's greatest conflict.

The remains of General Hogg were disinterred from Mount Holly School House in 1918. Only parts of his decomposed remains were recovered, along with buttons from his clothing. They were placed under this beautiful monument in Fort Robinette which stands in his honor.

CONFEDERATE CEMETERY
VICKSBURG

Maj. Gen. John Stevens Bowen
Brig. Gen. Isham Warren Garrott
Brig. Gen. Martin Edward Green

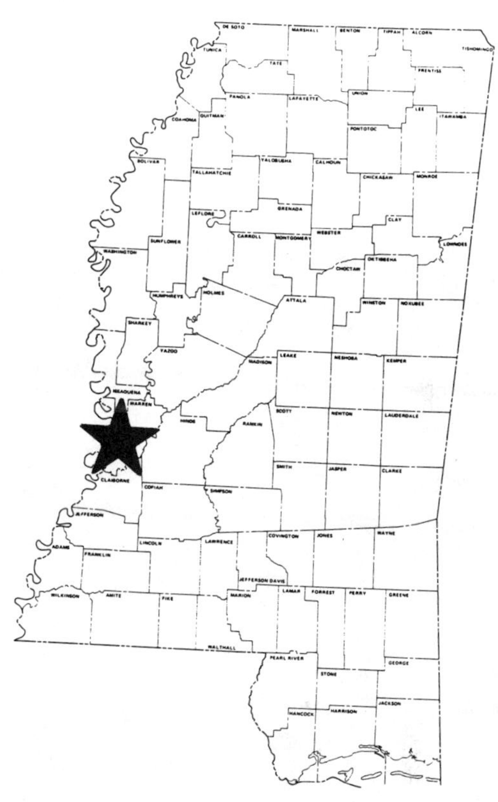

"Jesus, Lover of my soul" ___
Flashed the guns beneath the sky,
Silent never grew their roll ___
"Let me to thy bosom fly."

"Hide me, O Saviour, hide" ___
Fiercer roared the battle's blast:
Faster flowed the crimson tide ___
"O receive my soul at last!"

"Other refuge have I none" ___
Sang the boy beneath the tree___
"Mother soon will be alone,
O support and comfort me."

"All my trust on thee is stayed" ___
Listen how the Minies sing___
"Cover my defenseless head
With the shadow of thy wing."

Sank the sun behind the town
Just beyond the battle plain,
And the moon looked coldly down
On the wounded and the slain.

Dead upon the field he lay,
Past the war god's mad control;
But his white lips seemed to say:
"Jesus, Lover of my soul."

T. C. Harbaugh

Turn off I-10 on exit 4B, (Clay Street).
Turn north on Mission 66 Road.

Maj. Gen. John Stevens Bowen, C. S. A.
1830-1863

The ominous, dark clouds of doom rolled low and heavy over the besieged confederate army in Vicksburg, Mississippi, on July 2, 1863. The strategically vital southern city had been under siege for six long weeks by General Grant's army and its gaunt defenders were down to eating mule meat and rats for sustenance. Major General John S. Bowen had the unpleasant and uncharacteristic task of convincing his commander, General John Clifford Pemberton, that the cause was hopeless and surrender under acceptable terms was in order. General Pemberton had always trusted General Bowen's judgment and skill and Bowen was in a good position to know because he had engaged General Grant's forces at Grand Gulf, then Port Gibson in early May after Grant's army crossed the river below Vicksburg on May 1, and had fallen back across Bayou Pierre and finally into Vicksburg to make a final stand. He had been commended for gallantry and promoted to major general as a result and was thoroughly familiar with his old friend Ulysses S. Grant and his unconventional approach to warfare. General Bowen also knew that Grant's army of over 75,000 was positioned such as to deny all means of escape or resupply into Vicksburg. General Bowen was also becoming physically weak from the malnutrition and the heavy burden of fighting that had been placed on his division.

General Pemberton convened a council of war and heard the eloquent argument of Bowen, supported by all but two of his generals and reluctantly accepted the inevitable. He dispatched General Bowen to General Grant to relay his proposal for capitulation. Bowen even arranged a meeting between the two commanders on July 3 and as talks began to break down he proposed a commission comprised of officers of both sides to work out final details. Thus, General Bowen and Captain L. M. Montgomery of the Confederate army and Major Generals McPherson and Smith of the Union army conferred for hours and worked out the agreement that upon surrender all Confederates would be paroled and pledged to cease all hostilities until properly exchanged at a future date.

General Grant accepted and later praised his old friend John Bowen for being the catalyst which effected the surrender without further effusion of blood but as Confederate troops began their exodus from Vicksburg, General Bowen could feel himself becoming weaker as the dreaded attack of dysentery began its deadly grasp.

He was dearly loved by his troops, especially those of the 22nd Mississippi who served under him by request, "The Rodney Guards", "DeSoto Rebels", "Lafayette Farmers", and "Pegues Defenders". Described by the Honorable Pat Henry of Brandon, Mississippi who served with Bowen;

"...he was essentially a military man, a thorough disciplinarian and tactician. By some he was considered a martinet. He was exacting and tireless in drilling and disciplining his troops, the beneficial effect of which was evinced on many battle fields. In camp and on field he handled his troops with great skill and ability."

General John Bowen was born in Savannah Georgia on October 30, 1830, was educated in Milledgeville, and later was appointed to the United States Military Academy at West Point. There he graduated in the class of 1853, ranking 13th in his class. From there he was assigned to Carlisle Pennsylvania then as a second lieutenant in the Mounted Rifles where he served on frontier duty. In an effort to follow his dream to become an architect he resigned his army commission in 1856 to settle in St. Louis, Missouri, and was there at the outbreak of the war, in strong sympathy with the Southern cause.

Bowen was initially appointed captain of a unit of Missouri State Militia, then served as chief of staff for General Daniel Frost. He became an early prisoner of war when Union General Nathaniel Lyon seized Camp Jackson, but was later released and exchanged whereupon he organized the 1st Missouri Infantry and was elected their colonel. He was appointed brigadier general in the Confederate army on March 14, 1862, serving under General Leonidas Polk in Kentucky. General

Bowen was severely wounded at Shiloh but returned to action in time to participate in all major battles leading to the siege of Vicksburg. He commanded a brigade made up mostly of Mississippians, the 6th, 15th, 22nd, and the "Mississippi Battalion of Sharpshooters" along with the 1st Missouri Regiment.

The dream of Major General John Bowen to become an architect would never be realized. As the long march from Vicksbug continued he became weaker and had to be carried in a wagon. His men became terribly concerned. They crossed the Big Black River and on the lower Edwards and Raymond road they sought refuge for the General in the farmhouse of a Mr. Carnes about seven miles southeast of Edwards known as "Valley Farm". By then the thirty two year old major general was too sick to recover and the death vigil began. He died there on July 13, the result of severe dysentery. A carpenter named Robert Dickson who lived nearby constructed a wooden coffin although there was no material to line it and no srews to fasten the top. His staff placed the emaciated, uniform clad body of their beloved commander inside and buried him in the nearby Bethesda Presbyterian Church cemetery along side the grave of Lt. Dismukes of Arkansas. In July, 1887, the body of General John Stevens Bowen was disinterred from its lonely location and brought to Vicksburg where, in a grave site selected by Mrs. Wright of the Ladies Confederate Cemetery Association, it was reinterred by Mr. Albert Arnold, undertaker and acting sexton of the Vicksburg Cemetery.

In a report from General Pemberton the following statement was made about General Bowen:

"I cannot close this report without a brief tribute to the memory of two of the best soldiers in the Confederate army. I refer to Maj. Gen. John S. Bowen and Brig. Gen. Martin Edward Green. Always faithful, zealous, and brave, they fell as became them, in the discharge of their duty..... General Bowen, having passed scatheless through the bloody scenes of Shiloh, Iuka, Corinth, Grand Gulf, Port Gibson, Baker's Creek, and Vicksburg, perished by disease on the march from Vicksburg to Jackson after the capitulation. I can utter no higher eulogium upon him than to say he always performed his duty and never avoided danger."

The Confederate monument in memory of John Stevens Bowen erected in the Confederate section of Cedar Hill Cemetery erroneously reflects the rank of Lieutenant General. General Bowen had just been confirmed as major general prior to the siege. His actual grave site is unmarked in the same cemetery.

Brig. Gen. Isham Warren Garrott, C. S. A.
1816-1863

Since the repulse of a gallant union charge on May 22, 1863, the city of Vicksburg had been under tight siege, the Confederate soldiers inside the perimeter of the siege had become very restless, not being able to give battle and with little food or comforts. Just after dawn on the 17th of June the commander of the 20th Alabama, Colonel Isham Warren Garrott, became so irritated with the mundane duty that in disgust he sprang to his feet, borrowed the nearest soldier's rifle and walked up to the skirmish line to assess the situation first hand. He carefully took aim into the union positions just across a narrow gap. Unknowingly he had been in the keen sights of a union sharpshooter from the time he first exposed himself. A sudden crack of rifle fire from the union lines immediately found its mark as the forty seven year old Colonel was violently knocked from his feet, the bullet having pierced his heart he died instantly, without a sound. For Isham Warren Garrott, the terrible war had ended. Lt. Colonel Edmund Pettus, a close friend of his fellow soldier (also brother of Governor John J. Pettus) found a suitable place for Colonel Garrott's burial, in the yard of Mary Fenning Smith where Tomil Manor on Drummond Street now stands. The funeral was conducted at midnight for security reasons by the chaplain of the Alabama brigade, his grieving comrades in ceremonial attendance. Mrs. Smith wrote later;

"I will ever remember vividly that midnight funeral.........My gentle timid little mother could not have found her voice, we were all so grieved at his heroic, sudden, sacrifice".

A few days later a dispatch was received bringing news of Isham Warren Garrott's promotion to brigadier general effective 28 May, 1863. He died before becoming aware of his promotion to general. Years later, General Garrott's remains were removed to the Confederate Cemetery where a monument now stands in his honor.

Born in Anson City, North Carolina in 1816, Garrott moved to Marion Alabama to practice law in 1840 after his graduation from North Carolina State University. He became a trusted statesman in Alabama, as a two term legislator, active southern separatist, member of the 1860 electoral college, and appointed by Governor Moore as Alabama's commissioner to North Carolina for secession matters. He wasted no time in forming a regiment after hostilities began, the 20th Alabama. They were his boys, he was their trusted colonel.

They were dispatched first around Confederate Mobile and saw garrison duty until 1863. The Vicksburg theater was their first real combat test. Fighting as part of General Edward Tracey's brigade, Garrott's 20th Alabama saw violent action around Port Gibson where General Tracey was killed and Garrott assumed command of the brigade. Then at Champion Hill they were heavily engaged and later fell back into Vicksburg as part of General Stephen Dill Lee's command.

Today the Confederate Cemetery holds his remains, in an unmarked grave, away from his adopted state of Alabama but close to the hearts of her people.

Solemn Confederate monument to the memory of General Garrott in the cemetery where his remains lie after being removed from the yard of Mrs. Smith.

Brig. Gen. Martin Edward Green, C. S. A.
1815-1863

He was somewhat daring and reckless in battle, a little arrogant, which was not unusual for a cavalry commander, and had already had several narrow brushes with death by the time of the Vicksburg siege. Martin Edward Green knew the pioneer life early when as a native of Fauquier County, Virginia, he set out at the age of 21 with his young wife to seek fortune and adventure. He traveled by wagon to Wheeling West Virginia, then by steamer to St. Louis, over to Lewis County again by wagon and set up a steam sawmill an instrumental and somewhat lucrative enterprise as the surrounding area developed. As emotions heated up prior to the hostilities of 1861, he found himself in an awkward political position since his brother James was a United States Senator and supported President Lincoln.

At the outbreak of the Civil War he followed his own personal passion and raised a regiment of Confederate cavalry later becoming known as "Green's Missouri Cavalry Regiment", reporting for duty to Major General Sterling Price. As their colonel, Greene led them at the capture of Lexington, and fought bravely at Elk Horn Tavern in Arkansas, (Pea Ridge). After being commissioned as brigadier general on July 21, 1862, Green led his troops forward at Iuka and Corinth where he also took command of Gen. Louis Hebert's troops culminating in the fight at Hatchie

Bridge. Leading a brigade under General John Stevens Bowen, his Missourians opposed General Grant's northward advance at Port Gibson and subsequently falling back with Bowen to the defense of Vicksburg.

As the siege wore on Green's men frequently exchanged gunfire with the opposing union forces. It was one such occasion on June 25, 1863, when General Green was slightly wounded and taken to the field hospital. Two days later, back at the skirmish lines, he was warned by one of his subordinates that enemy sharpshooter activity had increased and to be careful whereupon he responded, "the bullet has not been molded that will kill me". A few moments later he walked up to a parapet to look at an enemy sap only 60 yards away. A sharpshooter drew down on General Green and fired the fatal shot, hitting him in the head, killing him almost instantly. Green's surgeon, John A. Leavy, mentioned the incident in his personal diary:

"Saturday, June 27, 1863, Forty-first day of the siege -This has been a sad day to us and our Missouri troops: the brave and good soldier, Gen. Martin E. Green was killed while at the parapet reconnoitering the position of the enemy. A minnie ball carried away a part of the occipital bone, just behind the right ear, and a large part of the brain with it. His remains were conveyed to my quarters, where suitable preparations were made for his funeral: we obtained a good coffin and gave it as good a funeral as possible: his remains were attended by mourning friends who sadly grieved at his loss."

The official records of the Union and Confederate armies states;

"On June 26, 1863, M. E. Green having been wounded the day before, was on this day unable to visit the fortifications and watch the movements of the enemy. On the morning of the 27th, he was in the ditches as was his custom, reconnoitering the positions of the enemy and while looking over the parapet in front of the enemy sap, which was only about 60 yards distance, he was shot through the head by a sharpshooter, and almost instantly killed."

He was buried in an unmarked grave in the Cedar Hill Cemetery in the George Marshall plot. The spot where he fell mortally wounded is marked in the Vicksburg National Military Park by a plaque near the Missouri monument. Later one of his men wrote; "Missouri lost her worthy son, General Martin Green, who fell bravely defending our works at Vicksburg, the last fortified post on "The Father of Waters", to furl the Stars and Bars.

General Pemberton said; " Always faithful, zealous, and brave, they fell as became them in the discharge of their duty. General Green feel upon the line he had so long and gallantly defended."

The monument in memory of General Green was erected in the Confederate section of Cedar Hill. His remains lie in an unmarked grave in the Marshall plot in the same cemetery.

OLD MACEDONIA CEMETERY
BLUE MOUNTAIN

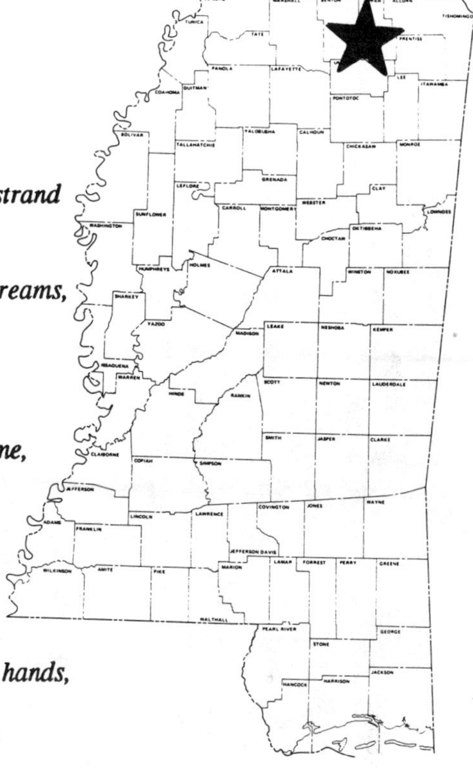

Brig. Gen. Mark Perrin Lowrey

I will sing you a song of that beautiful land,
The far-away home of the soul,
Where no storms ever beat on the glittering strand
While the years of eternity roll.

O, that home of the soul, in my visions and dreams,
Its bright jasper walls I can see.
Till I fancy but thinly the veil intervenes
Between the fair city and me.

That unchangeable home is for you and for me,
Where Jesus of Nazereth stands.
The King of all kingdoms forever is he,
And he holdeth our crowns in his hands.

O, how sweet it will be in that beautiful land,
So free from all sorrow and pain,
With songs on our lips and with harps in our hands,
To meet one another again!
Ellen N. Gates

From highway 15 turn west on West Main Street, then North on 1st Street and proceed two miles.

Brig. Gen. Mark Perrin Lowrey, C. S. A.
1828-1885

It was the usual busy Friday morning in the depot station in Middleton, Tennessee, on February 21, 1885. The depot agent, Mr. Mahaffey, was talking to a six foot three inch tall distinguished looking gentleman who had just purchased tickets for ten lovely young ladies and two of their teachers for rail passage to New Orleans to attend the Cotton Exposition. The tall slender man with piercing eyes was Brigadier General Mark Perrin Lowrey, founder and President of Blue Mountain Female Institute (presently Blue Mountain College) and highly touted Civil War general commonly referred to during the war as "the fighting parson of the Army of Tennessee". His countenance was striking, and his tranquil demeanor captivating as he was assured by Mr. Mahaffey that the students and their escorts were in good hands. He planned to ride with them as far as Grand Junction, Tennessee, then return to his beloved family and educational institution in Blue Mountain, Mississippi.

Suddenly, without any prior hint that anything was wrong, he staggered backwards, fell to the floor, breathed one last time and lay still forever. The spirit had yielded up its earthly burdens, leaving behind an enduring legacy of devotion and achievement. His life spanned a unique time of our nation's history, filled with uncertainty, temptation and difficulty, but overcoming all these he commanded the greatest respect and as one editorialist described him; "....... as a brave and intrepid soldier, as a fearless and skillful general on the battlefield, as a clear and able writer, as a preacher of the gospel, as a father and good citizen, and as a peerless Christian gentleman, Mark Perrin Lowrey came nearer fulfilling the standard of a perfect man than any other man whom we have ever known."

As a child he grew up in a large impoverished and uneducated family, yet his burning desire to someday become wealthy was surpassed only by his insatiable quest for education. His father, an Irish immigrant, died when Mark was a small boy and his mother, reflecting the strength so common among southern pioneer women, raised Mark and his ten brothers and sisters through great adversity.Answering the call to arms during the Mexican War in 1846, he became well versed in the valuable military skills of discipline, organization and tactics while serving under Colonel Charles Clark (later General Clark of Civil War fame and Governor of Mississippi).

After the Mexican War, bowing to a stronger calling than that of the pursuit of wealth, Mark Perrin Lowrey entered the ministry. While simultaneously ministering to two Baptist churches in Kossuth and Ripley, the twenty four year old pastor availed himself of every opportunity to gain education, directing his tireless energies to the pursuit of knowledge under the tutor of the educated among his congregations. However, he could not help becoming engulfed in the great tide of emotion surrounding the politics of secession in 1861, and because of his prior military experience his congregations and community implored him to form a regiment to "stand between our homes and the enemy". At first he had no intention of taking up arms, but the emotions of the time made it clear to him that in 1861, churches had less use for pastors than for fighting men, and more importantly he truly believed in the cause. Many mothers and fathers earnestly begged him to go with their sons who were being organized into local regiments. Thus he began his distinguished role as a prolific civil war commander, accepting the colonelcy of the 4th Regiment of state volunteers for sixty days duty, then later organizing the 32nd Mississippi Infantry in April, 1862.

Colonel Lowrey's 32nd Mississippi Infantry was organized in Corinth too late to be engaged at Shiloh although they performed many support duties during the battle. During his first combat engagement at Perryville, Kentucky, he was placed in command of the entire brigade when the brigade commander, General Sterling Wood, was wounded. While leading the subsequent assault General Lowrey himself was painfully wounded in the left elbow, a wound that disabled him for eight weeks necessitating his being sent home to recuperate. He secretly rejoined his wife and family in a little cabin a few miles south of Ripley, which at the time was controlled by Union forces. There, even during his convalescence and with the help of a young teenage spy named Fanny Fitzgerald of Kossuth, he continued to reconnoiter the enemy and gained valuable information on the troop strength in and around Corinth and Northeast Mississippi. After his arm was adequately healed Mark Perrin Lowrey knew that it was his duty to return to lead his men. According to his twelve year old daughter, Modena, (who later became affectionately known as "Mother Berry", as principal and vice president of Blue Mountain College) he gathered his wife and nine children at the door to tell them goodbye. "I remember that morning just as well as if it were yesterday," Mother Berry said. "A little negro boy stood at the door, holding father's horse. We children formed a circle around father, the twins in the cracker boxes that served as their cradles. Father took out his bible and read to us from the 121st Psalm.

"I will lift up mine eyes unto the hills from whence cometh my help. My help cometh from the Lord, which made heaven and earth. He will not suffer thy foot to be moved: he that keepeth thee will not slumber.... The Lord shall preserve thee from all evil: he shall preserve thy soul."

Then he kissed them, mounted his horse "Old Rebel" waived good-bye and rode off. They would not see him again for three long years.

At Chickamauga he was again in command of the brigade of Mississippians and he led a gallant charge through an open field on the most exposed part of the line. Observing this charge, General Pat Cleburne remarked "this is the bravest man in the Confederate Army." Mark Perrin Lowrey was promoted to brigadier general after the Chickamauga Campaign and fought brilliantly at Missionary Ridge where he rescued the First Arkansas Regiment just prior to their being overrun. At Dalton, Georgia, New Hope Church and Resaca, Lowrey's brigade fought gallantly. At Kennesaw Mountain, he mounted the breastworks, walking up and down the line in the midst of heavy fire to encourage his men. Seeing the many wounded of both sides lying in the field being threatened by a grass fire that had been started by cannon shot, he raised a white flag, the firing ceased on both sides. In one of the many strangely compassionate gestures of the war, he went forward and joined men from both sides in removing the wounded from the path of the fire, then they returned to their original positions and both sides reinstated hostilities.

He fought unscathed through the bloody battle of Franklin although engaged in some of the most intense fighting. Later in the Battle of Nashville his beloved horse "Old Rebel" that he had ridden throughout the war was shot from under him. He quickly mounted another horse and led on. Looking back he saw his faithful horse feebly trying to follow, but being unable to jump over a log, lay down to die. General Lowrey recalled not being able to hold back tears as he fought on through the battle.

General Lowrey had the unique combination of warrior and minister. As one of his men once said, "he could preach like Hell of Sunday, and fight like the devil the rest of the week". Actually he preached to his men almost every night. It was a common scene for the men to be gathered in large numbers around their campfires listening to the eloquent preacher. Many would listen to him who would not hear their chaplains. The General would baptize men by the dozens in the nearest river or creek. Accounts of General Lowrey's campsite sermons describe the fighting parson standing in his tall imposing countenance proclaiming;

"behold I stand at the door and knock: if any man hears my voice and opens the door, I will come in to him and will sup with him and he with me:
"call upon me in the day of trouble: I will deliver thee and thou shall glorify me."

A reporter for the Montgomery Newspaper filed the following account while touring Confederate bivouacs near Atlanta:

"We have had the pleasure of listening to a very impressive and eloquent sermon from Brigadier General Lowrey. The General is a man of superior acquirements, and is always heard with increasing interest. A faithful soldier of the Cross, as well as of his country, devout and brave, he unites, more than any living man, perhaps, those cardinal virtues of mind and heart which combine to make the noble, true, and conscientious Christian warrior."

It would have been easy for Mark Perrin Lowrey to parlay his military fame and respect into pursuit of wealth after the war, but instead he continued his ministry and became the state evangelist. He was offered on more that one occasion a Congressional seat by the State Legislature. He was highly recruited to run for Governor. He was offered numerous high offices by appointment. He turned them all down for his ministry. In a quest to find educational opportunities for his own children and many of those who did not have the opportunity, he founded the Blue Mountain Female Institute which flourished under his leadership and grew into a highly respected educational Institution in Mississippi.

So on Friday Morning, February 21, 1885, the heart that suddenly stopped beating in the railroad depot in Middleton, Tennessee, was not a normal heart. It was a brave, fearless, and dedicated one which held unconditional love for the men he led in the war, the congregations to which he ministered, the family for which he provided, the many whom were afforded the opportunity of education because of his efforts, and his thousands of dear friends. His death was met with great sadness throughout the state and south.

After the body was prepared in Middleton, a special funeral train was outfitted and the body was brought to Ripley, sadly accompanied by the ten students and their escorts Miss Maggie Tate and Miss Etta Berry. The train arrived in Ripley at 11 A. M. and the body of General Lowrey was taken to the Hines House where hundreds of friends paid their last respects while Miss Etta Berry and M. L. Marmon rode to Blue Mountain to break the news of the General's death to his family. On Sunday afternoon, February 23, 1885, at 2 p.m., General Mark Perrin Lowrey's funeral was held in the Blue Mountain Baptist Church with Dr. Finley delivering a stirring eulogy charging all to emulate his good works and righteousness. The thousands of mourners proceeded to the Macedonia Cemetery atop a beautiful hill that overlooks Tippah County where he was laid to his final rest A stately, tall monument was later placed at the head of General Lowrey's grave by his students and stands today as a striking reminder of one who lifted himself out of poverty to stand so tall for his beliefs and commitments during a time of great turmoil and strife.

General Lowrey's remains lie next to his wife underneath this majestic monument to his memory in Old Macedonia Cemetery near the educational institute he founded.

ODD FELLOWS CEMETERY
ABERDEEN

Brig. Gen. Samuel Gholson
Brig. Gen. John Gregg

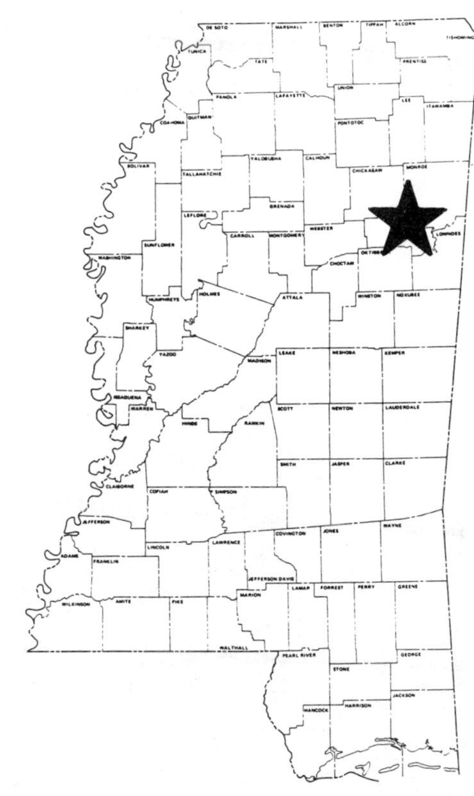

Where shall their dust be laid?
On the mountain's starry crest,
Whose kindling lights are signals made
To the mansions of the blest?
No! No! No!
For bright as the mountain be,
It has no gem in its diadem
Like the life spark of the free.

Where shall their dust be laid?
On the ocean's stormy shore,
With wailing woods, at their backs arrayed,
And shouting seas before?
No! No! No!
For deep as the waters be,
They have no depth like the faith which fired
The martyrs of the free.

Where shall their dust be laid?
By the valley's greenest spot
As it ripples down in leaps of shade
To the blue forget-me-not?
No! No! No!
For green as the valley be,
It has no flower like the bleeding heart
Of the heroes of the free.

Or where muffed pageants march
Through the spired and chiming pile
To the chancel rail of its oriel arch
Up the organ-flooded aisle?
No! No! No!
For grand as the minsters be,
They could never hold all the knightly hosts
Of Jackson and of Lee.

Where shall their dust be laid?
In the urn of the human heart,
Where its purest dreams are first displayed
And its passionate longings start?
Yes! Yes! Yes!
By memory's pictured wave
Is a living shrine for the dead we love
In a land they died to save.
A. J. Requier

One mile southeast of town on Poplar Street.

Brig. Gen. Samuel Jameson Gholson, C. S. A.
1808-1883

On memorial days and other special occasions when Civil War veterans would congregate in Aberdeen, Mississippi, a gray bearded old soldier conspicuously led the parade while wearing a sash, walking with a wobbly gate, and dangling an empty right sleeve. His aging body had been shot up badly in the Civil War; the right lung at Fort Donelson, the left leg at Corinth, a shoulder defending Jackson, and finally the right arm which he left at Egypt, Mississippi during his last battle.

He was Sam Gholson, former Federal Judge, U. S. Congressman, State Legislator, states rights advocate who had been a member of the 1860 Democratic Convention and Mississippi secession convention in 1861, and hard fighting brigadier general in the Confederate Army who fought in Chalmers' division, Nathan Bedford Forrest's Corps.

Gholson had been a resident of Aberdeen since 1840, when he and his wife, the former Margaret A. Ragsdale of Athens, Mississippi, purchased the magnolia shaded north half of the block bordered by Monroe, Columbus, High, and Hickory streets. They built a beautiful home which has since burned on that large lot. He was not a native Mississippian, having been born near Richmond, Madison County,

Kentucky, on May 19, 1808. Sam Gholson moved with his family to northern Alabama at the age of nine and later studied law at Russelville under the tutelage of Judge Peter Martin. After his admission to the bar he settled in Athens, Mississippi, the Monroe County seat, to begin his practice.

Reuben Davis beat him in 1835 in the race for prosecuting attorney but Sam Gholson demonstrated his tenacious spirit as he was elected to the House of Representatives the same year. Then an unique opportunity presented itself. Congressman David Dickson died while in office and Sam Gholson was elected to fill his unexpired term ending March 4, 1837. It was a stormy time in Washington for Gholson. On one occasion a heated debate with Congressman Henry A. Wise of Virginia over seating credentials almost resulted in a duel between the two men but was narrowly prevented by John C. Calhoun.

Sam Gholson was appointed Judge of the United States Court of Mississippi in 1838, by President Martin Van Buren, a position in which he honorably served for twenty two years. After secession in 1861, Gholson resigned his federal judgeship and instead of going to the bench of the Confederate District of Court of Mississippi, enlisted as a private of the Monroe Volunteers, then was elected their captain. They later became Company I, 14th Mississippi Infantry. Very shortly afterwards Sam Gholson was promoted to colonel, then brigadier general of State troops.

He saw action very early in the war. At Fort Donelson in support of General Albert Sidney Johnston's forces, he took a bullet in his right lung, almost fatally, and was captured with his troops upon the surrender of the fort. Upon his recovery in 1862, he was exchanged and by the summer was in the field again with his newly organized L Company of the 43rd Mississippi Infantry. As captain of this company he was part of Major General Sterling Price's forces in the Battle's of Iuka and Corinth where Gholson was again wounded. According to a newspaper account;

"....in the fierce battle of Corinth he drew his sword and was flourishing it. While thus engaged an enemy bullet hit the sharp edge of the sword and was literally split in two. Both parts were, of course deflected from the original course, one of the halves imbedding itself in the Captain's leg just above the knee."

Continuing service in the State forces he was commissioned major general in 1863, then on May 8, 1864, was commissioned brigadier general in the regular Confederate Army and placed in command of a cavalry brigade in Nathan Bedford Forrest's Corps, assigned to the First Division, commanded by General James Chalmers. In the battle to defend Jackson he was again painfully wounded, then was highly commended for gallantry in the Atlanta campaign. His daring cavalry continued to fight in the Tennessee campaign and after their retreat into Mississippi were thrown against the advance of Union Brig. Gen. Benjamin Grierson's cavalry in their objective to destroy the Mobile and Ohio railroad in Mississippi during December, 1864 and January, 1865. Gholson's riders temporarily checked Grierson at Egypt, Mississippi in December and fought with great determination and courage. It was there that General Gholson was wounded so severely he had to be left behind and again he fell into Union hands. Even though General Grierson and Colonel Joseph Karge both reported General Gholson to be mortally wounded he again survived. According to one account of the battle:

"General Gholson, with 250 mounted men, skirmished against the advance of General Grierson's raiders from Memphis on the Mobile and Ohio Railroad in December, 1864, falling back through Okolona and meeting reinforcements at Egypt, 700 men under Lieutenant Colonel Burke and King's Battery mounted on flat cars, from Mobile. They were attached at Egypt, on the morning of December 28. General Grierson, with the Fourth Missouri Cavalry, attacked Gholson's command behind a railroad embankment and was held in check until a charge was made by the Fourth Illinois Cavalry. General Gholson was wounded with 15 or 20 others of his command, and a number captured. Burke took position in a stockade and after a stubborn fight, in which Karge's Brigade had 90 killed and wounded, was compelled to surrender with 500 men. General Gholson was left at Egypt by General Grierson, with 35 or 40 severely wounded of the Second New Jersey Cavalry, under the care of Surgeon Krauter of that regiment."

When Surgeon Krauter amputated the wounded right arm of General Sam Gholson at Egypt, Gholson's career as a combat soldier had come to an end at the age of 57. He returned to his home in Aberdeen, was paroled, and after the war resumed his practice of law. He was again elected to the State Legislature, became Speaker of the House from 1865 to 1870, and entered for another term in 1878.

Then age finally began to catch up with the old warrior. In his obituary it was stated;

"..for many months he has stood at the margin of the grave confronting disease and debility and a will power that was almost proof against their cruel attacks; but the nerve that was iron a few years ago had succumbed to the combined assaults of time and disease, an the ripe sheaf yielded to the sythe."

General Samuel Jameson Gholson died at his home in Aberdeen on October 16, 1883, at 6 p.m., at the age of 76. His funeral at the Presbyterian Church at 3 p.m on the 18th was largely attended, all businesses in Aberdeen closed, as they paid final tribute to their fallen leader with interment in Odd Fellows Cemtery.

Stately monument at the head of the grave of General Gholson in Odd Fellows Cemetery.

Brig. Gen. John Gregg, C. S. A.
1828-1864

It was October 7, 1864, only six months from the end of the Civil War and Brigadier General John Gregg, though previously wounded, had almost made it through. He missed his loving wife, Mary. But there was yet another battle to fight and on this day it was raging along the Charles City Road below Richmond and the fighting Texas brigade commanded by General Gregg was heavily engaged. They had been driving the enemy back all morning and steadily gaining control of the field. Becoming concerned about the risk of extending his brigade too far in advance of supporting forces, General Gregg sent a courier staff officer, John F. Green, to the rear to find his corps commander General R. H. Anderson and ask for further instructions. Upon receiving the query General Anderson replied to the courier; "say to General Gregg, sir, press the enemy." At the receipt of Anderson's directive General Gregg continued pressing the attack while the enemy continued offering stiff resistance from their rear guard while in orderly retreat. Then the worst happened. In less than twenty minutes of receiving General Anderson's order to "press the enemy", thirty six year old General John Gregg lay dead on the roadside near New Market having taken a taken a "minie ball" in the neck while leading his brigade in the attack.

John Gregg was a very educated man, a mathematics professor who studied law in Tuscumbia, Alabama. He moved to Texas in 1852, and was elected district judge while living in Fairfield, in Freestone County. As a member of the Texas Secession Convention this highly respected Texan became a member of the Provincial Congress of the Southern Confederacy in Montgomery, Alabama, and later Richmond, Virginia, and was a member of the convention which adopted the Confederate Constitution. After Manassas Gregg resigned his Congressional seat in order to recruit a regiment of infantry in Texas and opted to command this regiment in the field.

Colonel Gregg and his 7th Texas infantry reached Fort Donelson in time to help in its defense but was among the large force which surrendered. He was taken prisoner, transported to Fort Warren, Massachusetts, near Boston and exchanged in September, 1862. Upon his release he was commissioned brigadier general, sent to Mississippi, and given command of a brigade consisting of the 3rd, 10th, 30th, 41st, 50th and 9th battalions of Tennesseeans as well as the reconstituted 7th Texas infantry.

General Gregg's brigade met the advance party of General Grant's forces at Raymond, Mississippi, on May 12, 1863, and fought so well that in his report General Grant described Gregg's force as two brigades. Gregg's aggressive combat brigade was also very conspicuous at Chickamauga where Gregg himself was severely wounded on September 19, 1863, and was out of action for several months. After his recovery he was assigned to the Army of Northern Virginia and given command of Hood's brigade of Texans where he gallantly fought on. On one occasion in the Wilderness on May 6, 1864, General Robert E. Lee rode out in front with Gregg to inspire and rally the troops prior to an attack. Gregg and his brigade of Texans refused to charge the enemy until the beloved commander of the Army of Northern Virginia agreed to go to the rear. General Lee reluctantly agreed and John Gregg's Texans made a ferocious charge into the foe.

When General Gregg was killed, his staff gathered around him and bid a sad farewell as his body was transported to Richmond. Funeral services were held there with President Davis and his cabinet in attendance. He was eulogized by General Robert E. Lee a few days later in general orders read to his Army as he reviewed them on parade. General John Gregg's body was embalmed and place in a vault owned by Mr. Sturdivant in Richmond to await further disposition by the family.

Mary Frances Garth Gregg was living with her father in Decatur, Alabama when she learned the terrible news of her husband's death, and was overcome with grief. She was a very unusual woman, a descendent of Patrick Henry and described as "a tall slender woman of military carriage and as firm in mind and character as her husband or any General for that matter.... she was a tender Christian woman." She had sometimes accompanied her husband in the field in the early days of the war and was no stranger to camp life, strong in spirit and stamina. Mary Garth Gregg so cherished her husband that, upon hearing of his death, she devoted her entire life's energy to the return of the General's body to a suitable final resting place where she could remain near him the rest of her life. Decatur, Alabama, however, was in enemy hands and she had to look elsewhere.

Her father owned some land near Aberdeen, Mississippi, and had a close friend there, Mr. Simon B. Sykes. So at the insistence of Mr. Sykes, Mary Gregg, accompanied by a faithful servant, left Decatur for Aberdeen, Mississippi, on a cold, bleak, December morning in 1864, hoping to find Aberdeen suitable as a final resting place for General Gregg. Passing through enemy lines and the rugged terrain of Lawrence, Winston, Walker, and Marion counties of Alabama and into Aberdeen, Mississippi, Mary Gregg found it to be a beautiful and peaceful setting with hospitable people and decided that it would be Aberdeen where she would bring the General's body and there remain for the rest of her life. She would need lots of help. It was late in the war and everything seemed to be coming unraveled but, relentlessly, Mary Gregg communicated with some of General Gregg's old friends, Postmaster General of the Confederacy John H. Reagan of Texas, and Secretary of War General John C. Breckinridge. With their help the following order was issued in Mobile assigning one of Simon Sykes relatives to assist Mary Gregg:

Special Order

"Sergt. E. L. Sykes of Company C., 16th Confederate Regiment, now stationed at Spanish Fort, is hereby detailed from his regiment and will at once repair to Aberdeen, Miss. and there join Mrs. General John Gregg, widow of the late General John Gregg of Texas, and proceed as her escort to Richmond, Va. Upon arrival at Richmond he will report to Gen. John C. Breckinridge, Secretary of War for further instructions.

Dabney H. Maury, Major General Commanding;
D. W. Foweree, Major and Adjutant General."

Sergeant Sykes went to Aberdeen, secured supplies, and on January 18, 1865, with Mrs.Gregg, began the hazardous journey to Richmond. Sergeant Sykes filed the following report upon their return.

"Our route from Aberdeen was to Meridian, Miss., via the Mobile and Ohio Railroad, thence to Selma, thence up the Alabama River to Montgomery. The journey thence to Atlanta and on to Richmond, via Greenville, Spartanburg, Charlotte, Salisbury, Greensboro, and Danville, was accomplished under many difficulties. The occupation of Atlanta in September, 1864, followed by sacking and burning November 15, 1864, preparatory to Sherman's march to the sea, had resulted in the tearing up of railroad tracks, rendering travel except by teams or march impossible. After surmounting many obstacles, journeying along the highways and byways, across swollen rivers, and over mountains, riding at times in the rude mountain conveyances of North and South Carolina or on horseback, the journey was brought to an end February 24, 1865, by our arrival in Richmond. The next day I accompanied Mrs. General Gregg to the War Department and reported to the Secretary, Gen. John C. Breckinridge, as directed in the order of detail. A visit was also made to Postmaster-General John H. Reagan, who aided materially in the preparation necessary for the return trip.

With the assistance of a detail made by the Secretary of War, preparations were begun for the removal of the body of General Gregg to Aberdeen, Miss. The heavy metallic case was taken from the vault, and, after being recoated with varnish and hermetically sealed, it was inclosed (sic) in a close-fitting wooden box. This box was reinclosed (sic) in a large outside box and the space between packed securely with charcoal and sprinkled with disinfectant, all under the supervision of surgeons of the army and officers with a detail of men. These preparations consumed several days, and when finally completed it was found that Mrs. Gregg was suffering too much from nervous prostration to start at once on the homeward bound journey. On March 8 the surgeon in attendance gave consent for Mrs. Gregg to leave, and the case was placed on a truck drawn by four horses and, under escort of cavalry and infantry detachments, conveyed to the depot and then placed on a train bound for Danville. From Danville we proceeded to Salisbury, N.C., where information of Sherman's movements in Georgia and South Carolina reached us. General Sherman had evacuated Savannah, Ga., on February 1, and with his army was marching through Georgia and South Carolina, leaving the country a barren waste. The Capitol at Columbia had been burned, and the people were fleeing before the Federal horde.

With these conditions confronting us, it was deemed advisable to change our route lest al plans should be frustrated by capture. Accordingly we left the railroad and, after being provided with wagon transportation by the Confederate government, proceeded across the country to Asheville, N. C., and there remained until more assuring news was had. We then continued our march overland to Union S.C., dismissed our wagon conveyance, and took a narrow-guage railroad to Spartanburg. We again had recourse to wagon transportation, making our way to Greenville, S.C. Along this route to Greenville Mrs. Gregg was again prostrated and was compelled to accept the hospitality of an old friend, Colonel Kenan, living at Kenansville, and was left behind.

They Sleep Beneath the Mockingbird

This brave, good woman, while bowed down with her grief, never ceased her appeals to me to hurry on to a place beyond the reach of the Federal army. Reaching Greenvlle, I was joined by the late Col. H. Clay King, of Memphis, Tenn., and a detachment under his command charged with a secret mission to the Trans-Mississippi Department.

At this point I was forced under orders of the quartermaster's department at Spartenburg to release the wagon transportation, and a local teamster with poor equipment undertook to convey the body to Washington, Ga., to which place we proceeded in company with Colonel King and his detachment. This portion of the journey was accomplished on foot, the condition of our team requiring it. Many difficulties were encountered along this route. Deserters and stragglers from the Army of Northern Virginia and form Johnson's army in North Carolina were crowding the highways in a mad effort to get beyond harm and to see the loved ones at home. One's life and belongings were not safe where these men roamed.

Reaching the Saluda River, we found the stream swollen from heavy rains and the river at every crossing lined with these same lawless characters. The ferryman was contending with them in their effort to seize the ferryboat and to put themselves across the stream, which was at flood tide. After seeking in vain to have these men give the right of way, Colonel King ordered his detachment to clear the ferryboat and guard the entrance until the funeral cortege could be ferried across the river. With our precious cargo on board, we put out into the stream. The swift current bore us rapidly downstream, and the boat was soon beyond control of the ferryman. Rapidly we passed beyond the appointed landing place. The possibility that the last resting place of this gallant soldier's body would be the bottom of the Saluda River nerved us all to renewed effort. Hastily improvising two additional oars from rude material for this emergency, we took turns in rowing, the ferryman steering the boat for the bank. Clinging to the overhanging willows skirting the bank, and after great effort, we pulled the ferryboat upstream half a mile to the usual landing place.

After this exciting incident we had no more trouble, and successfully reached Washington, Ga., where we rested for the night. We secured another local conveyance to Covington, Ga., but on reaching that point on the Georgia Railroad we found that with the evacuation of Atlanta November 15, 1864, this section of the railroad had been torn up, and we were forced to continue our march on to Atlanta forty miles distant. Approaching the city on the afternoon of April 2, 1865, we beheld in the distance the blackened walls and smokeless chimneys of the Empire City of the South, giving mute evidence of the vandalism of Sherman and his horde when he commenced his march to the sea. Lodging was obtained after much effort, and, weary from travel and anxiety, we found in sleep a much needed rest.

On the morning of April 3, we found the city in dire confusion. rumors of the collapse of the Confederacy were heard on every hand, and here, as elsewhere,the stragglers and deserters were robbing and plundering whenever opportunity offered. Upon presentation of the order from the Secretary of War, railroad transportation was furnished by the government quartermaster to Montgomery, Ala., and upon arrival at that point passage was taken on the government steamer Commodore Farad to Mobile, where we arrived on April 6, to find Gen. Dabney Maury, in command, preparing to evacuate the city, which was done on April 12, 1865. The services of an undertaker and embalmer were secured, and a thorough overhauling of the case was made. The outside box of poplar had absorbed the rain until the weight of the case had increased to fourteen hundred pounds.

Leaving Mobile on April 7, over the Mobile and Ohio Railroad, at Meridian we parted company with Colonel King and his detachment. On the morning of April 8 we left the train at Prairie, Miss., and, with the case in a wagon drawn by four stout mules, we proceeded to Aberdeen, eight miles distant. Ten days later the faithful wife of General Gregg arrived in company with Col. John W. Daney, of Texas, to find that the interment of her husband's body in Aberdeen had been successfully accomplished.

On April 28, 1865, I rejoined my command, which had retired upon theevacuation of Mobile to Gainsville, Ala., and there on May 24, 1865, thecommand formally surrendered to Maj. Gen. E.R.S. Canby, U.S.A. and eachsoldier received his parole."

So Mrs. Mary Garth Gregg settled in Aberdeen and for the next thirty three years she made her home in what is now known as the Gregg-Hamilton home not far from the Odd Fellows Cemetery where General Gregg was buried. She became a successful planter and one of Aberdeen's leading and most prominent and respected citizens. It was said of her that; ".. around her fireside there always sat a group of girls some deaf, some deficient but many who had no handicap except that of being orphans. Mrs. Gregg mothered them as she mothered her church and her town."

This noble lady never left the town in which her husband's remains were interred. She died in 1877, and was buried next to him in a solemn ceremony. Researchers often seem baffled about the grave of the brave and beloved Texan, General John Gregg, being located in Aberdeen, Mississippi. But as you walk through the historic cemetery there and observe the peaceful serenity of the two silent graves side by side near the beautiful monument erected by the citizens of Aberdeen, you somehow feel that he is at home, at last where he would have wanted to be, by the side of his faithful and endearing wife Mary who held for him love so timelessly and unconditonally that she refused to be parted from him, even in death.

The matching grave sites of General and Mrs. Gregg in Aberdeen under the statue of an angel. General Gregg's inscription reads, "Brig. Genl. Gregg, who fell in defence of Richmond"

MAGNOLIA CEMETERY
MAGNOLIA

Brig. Gen. Evander McNair

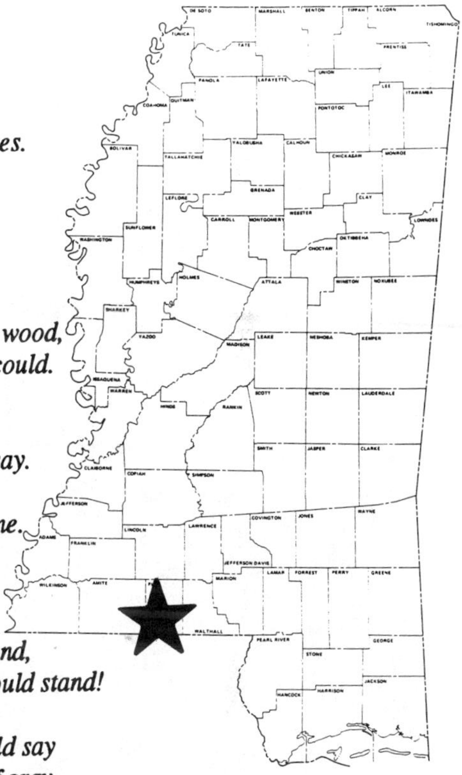

With a limp and a cane in has last waning days,
A bearded old soldier walked past rows of graves.
Confederate flags waved row by sad row,
As he thougth of the men that he led long ago.

The din of fierce battle in the face of the foe,
Roar of hot cannon as onward they'd go.
The charge up the crest, through the thick of the wood,
The shrill rebel yell that convinced them they could.

The smell of wet horses on a hot summer day,
And cries of young soldiers with limbs shot away.
Sparkling of campfires, the hardtack and pone,
A tear for the loved ones they thought of at home.

Long shoeless marches, the slow chilly rain,
Shouts of elation when victory was gained.
The sound of "Old Dixie" from strings of the band,
The sight of "Marse Robert" when all men would stand!

Then he thought of the future - what others would say
When he lies with his comrades in his jacket of gray.
Would they read the rich history and then understand,
Why they fought long ago for their dear cherished land?

For home and for hearth - the Constitution- not slaves,
More State's independence from government ways.
For dear sons and daughters, their honor and rights,
And strong Southern values on clear Southern nights!

H. A. Cross

From Interstate 55 take exit 10 (east) into the City of Magnolia, then turn south on Prewitt Street.

Brig. Gen. Evander McNair, C. S. A.
1820-1902

In the Hattiesburg, Mississippi home of his son-in-law, Dan Fairly, on November 13, 1902, the battered and rugged eighty-two year old Civil War General Evander McNair lay comatose, about to release his feeble grip on a long and accomplished life, his children, Edward, Myra, and Maggie keeping vigil at his bedside. His earthly tenure was coming to an end after several weeks of deteriorating health, not on the chaotic battlefield where he had risked life and limb in two separate wars, but in the warmth of home in the late winter of life amidst the placid adoration of his lineage. The commander who fought in two wars breathed his last at 9 p.m., his soul taking flight to "fame's eternal camping ground".

The long and eventful life began on April 15, 1820, in Richmond County, North Carolina, close to the little village of Laurel Hill. When his parents moved to Wayne County, Mississippi, Evander McNair was only one year old and spent his childhood in the frontier settlements of Wayne and Simpson Counties. As a young adult he pursued a livelihood in the mercantile business in Jackson, there volunteering for service in the war with Mexico in 1846, with Company E of the 1st Mississippi Rifles, pursuant to the call from their commander, Lt. Col. Jefferson Davis. While rising to the position of orderly sergeant in that regiment he was a combatant in several engagements of that war including the famous battle of Buena Vista. Although returning to his mercantile business in Jackson after very notable service, McNair eventually relocated to Washington,Arkansas, expanding his trade and marrying Miss Hannah Merrill of New York, a lady of very refined culture.

At the outbreak of the Civil War utilizing his recognized military training, Evander McNair quickly organized a battalion consisting of seven companies which joined with other regiments to constitute the Fourth Arkansas Infantry of the Confederate States Army with McNair as Colonel. Fighting under McCulloch's Division of General Earl Van Dorn's command, Colonel McNair led his troops through the Battle of Elk Horn then on to the defense of Corinth with Van Dorn and into Southeastern Kentucky where, at Richmond, with Major General Kirby Smith, he was wounded while commanding a brigade in the fierce engagement against the forces of Union General Manson, completely routing them. As a result, General Kirby Smith, who witnessed the amazing performance of McNair and his brigade, bestowed upon him a battlefield commission to brigadier general for "the excellent management of his brigade in this battle, as well as for the gallant manner in which his troops broke the line of the Federals and put their whole force to the rout". This commission was later confirmed by the Confederate Congress in Richmond to rank from November 4, 1862.

Under Maj. Gen. John P. McCown's division of Hardee's Corps, General McNair's brigade fought in the Battle of Murphreesboro on December 31, 1862, then with Joseph E. Johnston in his futile attempts to relieve Vicksburg. He was painfully wounded in the thigh at Chickamauga, but recovered in time to participate with General Price in the famous "Missouri Raid".

At the end of the War with the south's economy in a shambles, General McNair attempted to re-establish his mercantile trade in Washington, Arkansas, but unable to do so he and his family removed to New Orleans, then to Magnolia, Mississippi. It was in Magnolia that he and his wife Hannah made so many dear friends as he marketed his trade in the old "Harry Hall" store and built their lovely residence on the upper section of Clark Avenue, later occupied by Dr. A. D. Felder. In Magnolia, Evander McNair's greatest tragedy happened, his loving wife Hannah died after a short illness in 1878 and was buried in the local cemetery. It was this cemetery in which General McNair wished to be interred at his death beside his cherished wife.

So they prepared his body in Hattiesburg, transported it to Magnolia, the beautiful little town south of McComb, and there held a solemn funeral service at the Presbyterian Church, officiated by the Reverend W. H. Perkins. Proceeding to the cemetery, they lowered the brave general into his final resting place next to his wife in the McNair plot in the west central portion of the lovely burial ground a long way from the men of the 4th Arkansas, and a long way from Hannah's native New York City, but in the heart of the deep South surrounded by true friends who shared strong belief in the cause to which he devoted every fiber of his existence to defend.

A single but grand monument in Magnolia Cemetery marks the grave of General Evander and Hannah McNair.

ODD FELLOWS CEMETERY
OKOLONA

Brig. Gen. William Feimster Tucker

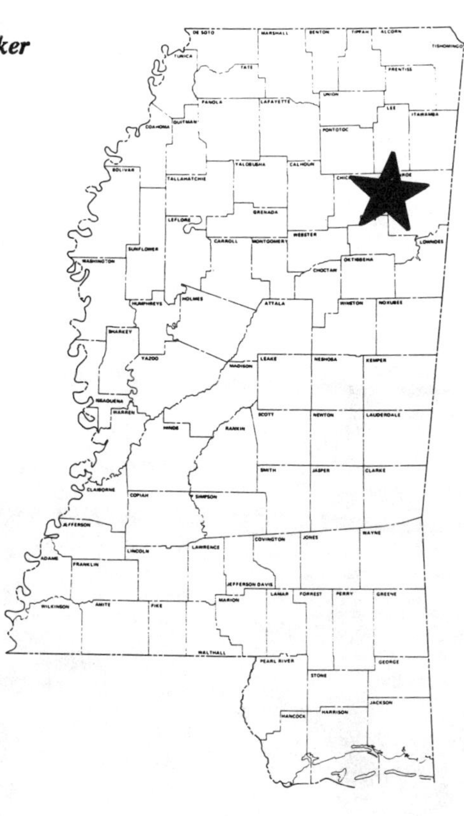

In their silent camps of glory,
Stretching ever far away,
Sleep the men who live in story,
Valiant wearers of the gray;
For them no drums are beating,
For them no bugles blow,
No advance and no retreating,
No fierce onsets of the foe.

In the robin-haunted thicket
Where the autumn leaves are blown
Sleeps the ever-watchful picket
In a glory all his own;
And the ring dove coos above him
At the gloaming of the day,
For the sake of those who love him
In his cerements of gray.

Nevermore for them the rattle
Of the muskets grim and dread,
Nevermore the horrid battle
Where the richest blood was shed;
Crown them all with gentle flowers
From the meadow and the dell,
They are sleeping through the hours
In the land the loved so well.

They will march again in splendor,
All transfigured, yet our own,
And each hero, each defender
To his comrades shall be known;
They shall rise again in glory,
Though they rest beneath the sod,
Gallant men of song and story
In the cantons of their God

T. C. Harbaugh.

Located North of Okolona on highway 45, turn east on Winter Avenue then south on Martin Luther King Drive.

Brig. Gen. William Feimster Tucker, C. S. A.
1827-1881

September 14, 1881, was a rainy and stormy Wednesday night in Okolona, Mississippi. After a long, busy day at his downtown law office General W. F. Tucker had retired to his home located about a mile northwest of town and 200 yards west of present day highway 45. After his evening meal with his family, he had a cup of tea, and met with two of his friends about some business matters. They left at about 9:00 p.m., and General Tucker finally settled down in his bedroom for his much needed rest But rest for the Tucker family and the citizens of Okolona would soon be transformed into confusion and terror by an assassin who quietly lurked in the rainy darkness just outside, stalking from window to window, waiting for his opportunity.

The general undressed and lay down across his bed. Earlier in the day he had been editing the next edition of the "Chickasaw Messenger" and, not being satisfied with it, he handed it to his wife Mary Josephine and asked her to read it and offer her opinion. As Mary left the room to read, General Tucker opened a letter from his son Hal who was in New Mexico. The moment the assassin was waiting for had presented itself- the fifty four year old general was alone in his room!

A faint tap was heard at the bedroom window and General Tucker got up, walked over, and peered out into the darkness. The telltale tracks left in the mud by the assassin indicated that he stepped back a few feet onto a little mound near the window. The general asked, "who's there?". The sudden crack of the pistol's report supplied the answer and signaled the flight of the projectile which penetrated General Tucker's chest just below the left nipple and traveled slightly upward into his heart rendering him unconscious almost immediately as his cardiovascular system rapidly lost its life sustaining pressure and Okolona and Mississippi lost one of their most trusted leaders. Mrs. Tucker came rushing in to find him lying dead in a pool of blood, the murderer gone from sight frantically seeking his cowardly escape.

Word spread rapidly about the general's death and within a half an hour the whole town was awake and along with the sheriff and his deputies launching an all out search for the assassin. Of immediate suspicion was a black man named Houston Parish, with whom General Tucker had an altercation a few days earlier and had struck with his cane because of Parish's alleged scolding and thrashing of General Tucker's son. Parish had been overheard asking for someone to sell him a pistol after the incident. After Parish was arrested and exonerated another man, Mr. Shaw came under suspicion. He was being exposed by General Tucker for misappropriation of a guardian trust fund and was accused of hiring two men to assassinate the general to cover up information that at the time only General Tucker was aware. Shaw and the two men were acquitted and the identity of the real assassin was never known.

General W. F. Tucker's funeral was held at 9:00 a.m. in Okolona on September 16, 1881, and his remains were followed to Odd Fellows Cemetery by almost all the population of the town both black and white. The Reverend Amos Kendall of Aberdeen conducted the services and a delegation from Aberdeen which attended included Hon. L. E. Houston, Hon. R. O. Reynolds, Capt. R. E. Houston, Hon. E. O. Sykes, Hon. E. H. Bristow, Major S. A. Johns, and Capt. E. H. Thompson.

The eulogy of William Feimster Tucker contained the chronology of his dedicated and untiring service to his fellow man. Born in Iredell County, North Carolina, on May 9, 1827, he was educated at Emory and Henry College of Virginia, and at the age of 21 he and his friend, Dr. J. Murdock, left their native Carolinas for adventure in the West. They settled in Houston, Mississippi, the county seat of Chickasaw County, a young frontier area being settled as part of the Chickasaw Cession of 1832. According to one of his close friends, J. R. McIntosh;

"He came without money, friends or influence, but he possessed those elements of character which were worth far more than money. He was generous, brave, courteous, just and honest."

They Sleep Beneath the Mockingbird

In Houston he was first employed as a teacher and pursued the study of law in his spare time. Upon admission to the Bar he began his practice in Houston, married Miss Mat Shackelford, daughter of Colonel Henry Shackelford, a wealthy and respected planter of the community, formed a partnership with Major T. S. Evans, another brilliant young lawyer of Houston, and was elected as Probate Judge of Chickasaw County.

Tucker was only 33 years old at the outbreak of the Civil War. He quickly went about the organization of a rifle company known as the "Chickasaw Guards", and by January, 1861, they had already deployed to Pensacola, Florida, where Captain Tucker established himself as a highly respected leader of his troops. They saw no action in Florida, but were later assigned to Virginia where they took part in the Battle of Manassass as part of General Benard Bee's brigade.

Seeing the need for additional troops, Tucker returned to Mississippi to organize the 41st Mississippi Regiment and was elected their Colonel on May 8, 1862. This regiment, constituted by the "Walker Pope Reserves", "Southern Rejectors of Old Abe", "Verona Rifles", and the "Mississippi Rip Raps", with Colonel Tucker as their commander saw action at Perryville, Murfreesboro, Chickamauga, and Chattanooga.

W. F. Tucker was promoted to brigadier general on March 1, 1864, commanding a brigade composed of the 7th, 9th, 10th, 41st, and 44th Mississippi Regiments. He was wounded four times in battle but the most serious was at Resaca, Ga. on May 14, 1864, when his arm was broken by a rifle shot incapacitating him for field command during the remainder of the war, and forever rendering his left arm useless. He served his final months of duty as commander of the southern district of Mississippi and East Louisiana, and there was instrumental in negotiating an end to hostilities in that area with Union Major General N. P. T. Dana.

General Tucker resumed his practice of law after the war settling in Okolona.

He was elected to the Mississippi Legislature in 1876, and in 1880 he came within a few votes of being nominated to Congress. He was a devoted and consistent member of the Methodist Church. In his eulogy, his law partner, the Honorable J. R. McIntosh also noted:

"..in every position in life which he was called to fill, he performed his duty faithful and well- whether as a school teacher, Judge, lawyer, soldier or legislator,... or in the church, he presented to the world the same illustrative character."

George M. Moreland of the Commercial Appeal referred to Tucker in an article on April 7, 1929:

"Every land has its hero. Rome boasts its gallant Horatius, who held the bridge as well; Carthage has its Hannibal; Greece is proud of its Leonidas and its Miltiades; Scotland preserves the story of its Robert Bruce, and England delights to tell the exploits of its Richard the Lion Hearted. So Chickasaw County has its hero too. When one visits the inviting old county its people will tell proudly of that doughty warrior's fame and over at the beautiful "City of the Dead" at Okolona they probably will point to the hallowed spot where his ashes are reposing."

General Tucker's distinguished monument at his grave in Odd Fellows Cemetery is testament to his distinguished and illustrious career in public service.

EPILOGUE

The thirty-three Mississippi grave sites that contain the remains of general officers of the Regular Confederate States Army should be permanently enshrined, if not in official archival designation then certainly in our individual hearts as monuments to the many thousands of brave men who poured out their last full measure of devotion to their beloved Southland and lie in unmarked and uncharted graves. These true leaders should reflect, even in death, the standard for the men they led with their shrines forever beaconing a constant reminder of the terrible costs exacted from the rupture of our nation's fabric of government in 1861, and the strength with which it was re-woven.

The 1860 Mississippi census records only 70,295 white males of military age yet the muster roles of the military units formed after 1861 bear the names of over 80,000 men from Mississippi who served in the conflict indicating the presence of very old men and very young boys involved in the carnage. In 1866, roughly twenty-five percent of the budget of the State of Mississippi was spent on the procurement of artificial limbs for veterans. Military occupation had replaced the proud democratic government which preceded the war which included some of the South's finest statesmen. Mississippi's proud pre-war Congressional delegation made up of Senators Jefferson Davis, and A. G. Brown, and Congressmen O. R. Singleton, L.Q. C. Lamar, Reuben Davis, William Barksdale, and John J. McRae were replaced post-war with commissioners scrambling to Washington seeking conditional reinstatement to the Union..

The agrarian economy of the State of Mississippi which was so plush prior to the war was in ruins, with almost all livestock gone as well as the availability of laborers. Markets had vanished and families pathetically separated, cities burned, the Governor imprisoned and martial law invoked. Yet from these seemingly hopeless ashes a new South slowly emerged, spiritually strong and economically vibrant, ready to enter the 21st century, with strong and forceful leadership indicative of the innate and unbounded human spirit so clearly reflected in the leaders who are the subject of this book.

The leaders of the Old South represented in this book did not make a stupid blunder, they took some very difficult decisions that leaders of today would most probably have taken if faced with identical circumstances and emotions. They settled an impasse in our constitutional framework, albeit with tragic carnage and suffering, that, left unresloved, most probably would have later caused the total collapse of our government. They were true heroes, tried and tested, with the same emotions as you and me, yet filled with character, resolve, fortitude, and extremely blessed with much more than the normal allotted measure of leadership.

They Sleep Beneath the Mockingbird

ACKNOWLEDGMENTS

Unbounded thanks is due my wife of twenty-five years, Carolyn, and our two precious sons Daniel and John without whose patience and understanding I could not have completed this work.

In addition, I will forever remain indebted to the following people who pointed me to the correct research trail, provided directions to local cemeteries and grave sites, allowed access to family files and genealogy, or simply offered kind encouragement:

Shelby Foote, Memphis; Elbert Hilliard, Ann Lipscomb, Elaine Owens, and Victor Bailey, Mississippi Department of Archives and History; Genevieve Barksdale, Ocean Springs; Catherine Morgan, Natchez; Lynn Houston and Lillian Mann, Evans Memorial Library, Aberdeen; Carolyn Mounce, Pam Pharr, and Mary Dean Hollis, Blue Mountain College; Sandra Harris, Office of the Webster County Chancery Clerk; Frances Jones and Marion McCain, Jones Grocery, Tomnolen; Mary Bell Pulaski, Columbus Public Library; Tom Lewis, Friendship Cemetery, Columbus; Norman Chaffin, Pond's Store, Wilkinson County; Murella Hebert Powell, Biloxi Public Library; Mike McDonald, Biloxi Cemetery; Terry Winschell, Vicksburg National Military Park; Dr. Jack D. Welsh, M. D., Oklahoma City, Oklahoma; Wallace Berry, Cedar Lawn Cemetery, Jackson; Donald Estes, Natchez; Margaret Green Rogers, City Museum, Corinth; Nancy Butler and Bell Batton, Harriette Person Memorial Library, Port Gibson; Donna Dye, Mississippi Historical Museum, Jackson; Tommy Weems, Maxey Phillips and Johnny Jones, Jackson.

APPENDIX A

CIVIL WAR BATTLES AND SKIRMISHES IN MISSISSIPPI

Corinth - April 8, 1862; May 17, 1862, and October 3, and 4, 1862.

Farmington - May 3, 1862.

Glendale - May 8, 1862.

Metamora - October 5, 1862.

Rienzi and Kossuth - August 26, 1862.

Iuka - September 19 and 20, 1862, and July 7 and 9, 1863.

Booneville - May 30, 1862, and July 1, 1862.

Blackland - June 4, 1862.

Ripley and Moscow Station - December 1 to 4, 1863.

Holly Springs - December 20, 1862, May 24, 1864, and August 27 and 28, 1864.

Hudsonvlle - November 8, 1862.

Davis Mills - December 21, 1862.

Hernando and Coldwater- April 18 and 19, 1863.

Rolling Fork - March 16 to 22, 1863, and September, 1864.

Dillon's Bridge - May 12, 1863.

Pontotoc - July 13, 1864.

Coldwater - September 10, 1862.

Harrisburg - July 14, 1864.

Coahoma County- August 2, 1862.

They Sleep Beneath the Mockingbird

Abbeville, Oxford and Hurricane Creek- August 7 to 14, 1864.

College or Oxford Hill - August 21 and 22, 1864.

Abbeville - August 23, 1864.

Yazoo City - July 13, 1863.

Yazoo City Expidition including Benton and Vaughn's - May 4, to 13, 1864.

Yazoo River Expedition - February 1 to March 8, 1864.

Franklin - January 2, 1865.

Jackson - May 14, 1863.

Jackson, Bolton Depot, Canton and Clinton - July 9 to 16, 1863.

Expedition from Vicksburg to Meridian with engagements at Champion Hill, Raymond, Clinton, Jackson, Decatur, Chunkey Station, and occupation of Meridian, Lauderdale and Marion- February 3, to March 5, 1864.

Summerville - November 26, 1863.

Hurricane Creek - October 23, 1864.

Source, Colonel W. D. Holder, Civil War Veteran.

Wyatts and Ingram's Mill - October 12 and 18, 1863.

Brice's Crossroads near Guntown- June 10, 1864.

Bay Springs, or Vincent's Cross Roads - October 26, 1863.

Egypt Station - December 28, 1862.

Prairie Station - February 1, 1863.

Coffeeville - December 5, 1862.

Grenada - August 13, 1863.

Fort Pemberton near Greenwood - March 13 to April 5, 1863.

Vicksbug, United States Fleet - June 26 to 29, 1862, siege May 17 to July 4, 1863.

Chickasaw Bayou - December 28 and 29, 1862.

Mississippi River below Vicksburg- February 24, 1863.

Champion Hill - May 16, 1863.

Big Black River - May 17, 1863.

Port Gibson - May 1, 1863.

Rodney and Port Gibson - December 17 to 26, 1863.

Coleman's Plantation - July 4 and 5, 1864.

Grand Gulf - April 29, 1863; July 16 and 17, 1864.

Natchez - May 13, 1862, July 8, 1863, and November 11, 1863.

Raymond - May 12, 1863.

Bolton and Birdsong Ferry- July 4, and 5, 1863.

Canton - July 17, 1863.

Canton, Brownsville and Clinton - October 15 to 18, 1863.

Near Canton - February 27 and 28, 1864.

They Sleep Beneath the Mockingbird

Appendix B

MISSISSIPPI REGIMENTS IN THE CIVIL WAR

According to the records of the War Department in 1897 the following Confederate organizations from Mississippi were listed.

Forty-nine Infantry regiments

Fifteen Infantry battalions

Twenty-four Cavalry regiments

Sixteen Cavalry batallions

One regiment Cavalry reserves

Seventeen regimnents State troops

Three batallions State troops

Eight batallions State Cavalry

One mixed regiment; Mississippi, Tennessee and Alabama

One mixed batallion; Mississippi, and Tennessee

One mixed cavalry batallion; Mississippi and Alabama

One partisan ranger regiment, One partisan ranger batallion

Five batallions sharp shooters

One artillery regiment

One artillery batallion

One artillery battery

The Jeff Davis Legion

Mixed Mississippi, Alabama, and Georgia cavalry (Harvey Scouts)

(source, letter from War Department to Col W. D. Holder, Nov. 6, 1897.)

They Sleep Beneath the Mockingbird

Bibliography

Adams, Daniel

"Death of Gen. Daniel W. Adams," The Semi-Weekly Clarion, Jackson, Ms., 18, 1872.

"Particulars of the Death of Gen. Daniel W. Adams," The New Orleans Times, June 14, 1872.

"Death of Gen. Daniel W. Adams," The Daily Picayune, New Orleans, Friday, June 14, 1872.

"The Funeral of Gen. Adams," The Daily Picayune, New Orleans, June 15, 1872.

Adams, William Wirt

"Brig. Gen. Wirt Adams," The Jackson Daily Clarion, December, 1, 1864.

"How the Deadly Fight Occurred," The Natchez Democrat, Thursday, May 3, 1888.

"John H. Martin", The New Mississippian, Jackson, Mississippi, May 8, 1888.

"Was a Witness to the Jackson Tragedy," The Natchez Democrat, Thursday, May 3, 1888.

"Tribute to Gen. Adams," The Clarion Ledger, Thursday, May 31, 1888.

"Reminiscences of Combats of Ante-Bellum Days," The Clarion Ledger, June 14, 1888.

Saggus, James, "William Wirt Adams, Unsung Hero of Civil War, Played Big State Role," The Clarion Ledger, Jackson, Ms., January 1, 1866.

Baldwin, William Edwin

"Brigadier General Edward Baldwin" The Mobile Register and Advertiser, Sunday Morning, February 21, 1864. (two articles).

Banks, Col R. W., "Famous Mississippians", article from unidentified newspaper contained in Baldwin File, Columbus, Miss. Public Library.

Mississippi Official and Statistical Register, 1908, pp. 571-592.

_ My Journal- Chambers

"Diary of General Claudius Wistar Sears", Sword Featherston file, Mississippi Archives and History, Jackson.

Barksdale, William

"The Burial of Gen. Barksdale," The Daily Clarion, Jackson, Ms. January 11, 1867.

"General William Barksdale," The Weekly Clarion, Jackson, Ms., January 17, 1867.

"Last Hours of General Barksdale," The Mississippi Index, Wednesday, June 13, 1866.

"Died, Mrs. Narcissa L. Barksdale," The Weekly Clarion, Jackson, Ms. March 31, 1875.

Hearn, Phil, "Barksdale Museum Exhibit Recalls General's Exploits," The Clarion Ledger, Jackson, Ms., Sunday September 22, 1968.

Winschel, Terrence J, "Their Supreme Moment: Barksdale's Brigade at Gettysburg," Gettysburg Historical Articles of Lasting Interest, July, 1989, pp. 70-77.

Letter from David Parker (Pvt., Co. C, 14 VT at Gettysburg) to Mr. Barksdale, dated 22 March 1882, State of Mississippi Department of Archives and History, Jackson, Ms.

Muffly, J. W., The Story of Our Regiment, Des Moines, 1904, (by Alfred Thorley Hamilton, Asst. Surgeon, 148 PA at Gettysburg), p. 173.

Marbaker, T. D., History of the 11th New Jersey Volunteers, Trenton, N.J. 1898, p. 98.

Letter to Rev. T.E. Teasdale from Samuel Taylor, dated March 28, 1865, concerning the undertaking procedures for the body of General Barksdale, Mississippi Department of Archives and History, Jackson, Ms.

Benton, Samuel

Rowland, Dunbar, Military History of Mississippi,

The History of Marshall County, The Garden Club of Marshall County, 1936.

"Benton, Samuel", Goodspeed's Biographical Memoirs of Mississippi, pp. 380-381.

Bowen, John Stevens

Brandon, Pat Henry, "Maj. Gen. John S. Bowen, C.S.A.", The Confederate Veteran, Vol. XXII, April, 1914, pp.171-172.

Chew, Phil, "Reunion of The Twenty-Second Mississippi", The Confederate Veteran, Vol.VII. Sept. 1899, pp.1-2.

"Grave of Maj. Gen. John S. Bowen", The Confederate Veteran, April, 1908, p.159.

Wells, W. Calvin, "Gen. John S. Bowen", The Confederate Veteran, Vol. XXI., December, 1913, p. 564.

Cotton, Gordon, A., "CSA Generals' Graves Remain Unmarked, Too", Vicksburg Evening Post, December 3, 1978.

Brandon, William Lindsay

"Gen. Wm. L. Brandon", The Daily Democrat, Natchez, Ms. Wednesday, August 13, 1890.

"W. L. Brandon" The Woodville Republican, Woodville, Ms. Saturday, August 16, 1890.

Interview with and various documents in possession of Ms. Catherine Brandon Morgan, Natchez, great, great grandaughter of General W. L. Brandon.

Biographical and Historical Memoirs of Ms. Vol. I., The Reprint Company Publishers, Spartanburg, S. C. 1978. pp. 420-422.

Letter to Mr. Perry from Robert L. Brandon, son of General W. L. Brandon, dated June 2, 1896, Brandon Subject File, Mississippi Department of Archives and History, Jackson.

Rowland, Dunbar, Mississippi, Vol. I, p. 293.

Brantley, William Felix

"The Brantley Asssassinations-The Causes Which Led to Them", The Semi-Weekly Clarion, Jackson, Miss., Nov. 15, 1870.

"Communicated", The Semi-Weekly Clarion, Nov. 18, 1870.

Eudy, Sen. J. E., "General Brantley", The Webster Progress, December, 20, 1951.

Rowland, Dunbar, Encyclopedia of Mississippi History, Biographical., Southern Historical Association, 1916. Vol. I, pp. 294

The Official and Statistical Register of the State of Mississippi-1908, Nashville, Tenn., Press of the Brandon Printing Company., 1908.

Clark, Charles

"Charles Clark-The Model Legislator, Judge and Military Chieftain", The Commercial Appeal, Memphis, Tenn., December 29, 1895.

"Captain Keller's Diary", The National Observer, Monday, October 8, 1962.

Boydstun, Carol, "Erosion Of Time Conquers Historic Mansion", The Commercial Appeal, Memphis, September 12, 1974.

Ogden, Sillers, "Charles Clark- State's War Governor and CSA General", The Clarion Ledger, Jackson, Miss. November 12, 1967.

Rowland, Dunbar, Enclyclopedia of Mississippi History, Biographical, Southern Historical Association, 1916. Vol. I, pp437-439.

Letter from Gen. E. D. Osband to Charles Clark, Esq., May 20, 1865, Charles Clark Subject File, Mississippi Department of Archives and History, Jackson.

Letter from Charles Clark, Governor, to General E. D. Osband, May 22, 1865,.Charles Clark Subject File, Mississippi Department of Archives and History, Jackson.

Davis, Joseph Robert

"Gen. Joseph R. Davis", The Biloxi Herald, Sept. 19, 1896.

"Gen. J. R. Davis- His Life and Work Written in the State's History", The Daily Picayne, New Orleans, September 17, 1896.

Winschel, Terrence J., "Heavy Was Their Loss: Joe Davis's Brigade at Gettysburg", Gettysburg: Historical Articles of Lasting Interest, Part I, January 1, 1990., Part II., July 1, 1990.

Dockery, Thomas Pleasant

"General Dockery", The Daily Democrat, Natchez, March 6, 1898.

"General Dockery", (announcement of death), The Daily Democrat, Natchez, March 2, 1898.

"Death of General Dockery", The Daily Democrat, Sunday, February 27, 1898.

Featherston, Winfield Scott

"Gen. Winfield S. Featherston", The Holly Springs South, Holly Springs, Miss., June 3, 1891.

"Convention of U. C. V. at Jackson", The Holly Springs South, Holly Springs, Miss., June 10, 1891.

"Featherstone for Governor", Editorial, The Pontotoc Observer, Pontotoc, Miss., July 4, 1885.

"General W. S. Featherstone for Governor", Editorial, The Pontotoc Democrat, Pontotoc, Miss. December 27, 1882.

Cole, Raymond, "Winfield Scott Fetherston", Featherston Subject File, Mississippi Department of Archives and History, Jackson.

Ferguson, Samuel Wragg

"General Ferguson to be Buried This Afternoon", The Daily Clarion-Ledger, Sunday, February 4, 1917.

"Military Honors Confederate Hero", The Daily Herald, Biloxi, Miss. February 6, 1917.

"Confederate Chief Taken by Death", The Daily Herald, Biloxi, Miss. February, 5, 1917.

"General S. W. Ferguson", Biographical and Historical Memiors of Mississippi, Goodspeed Publishing Co., Chicago, 1891, Vol. I, pp. 732-733.

Garrott, Isham Warren

Letter from Mary F. Smith, located in regimental file, 20th Alabama, Vicksburg National Military Park.

"Five Confederate Generals died in Vicksburg's defense", Siege, The

Vicksburg Evening Post, summer, 1988.
Cotton, Gordon A., "CSA Generals' Graves Remain Unmarked, Too", The Vicksburg Evening Post, Vicksburg, December 3, 1978.

Gholson, Samuel Jameson
"Death of Gen. S. J. Gholson", The Aberdeen Examiner", Aberdeen, Miss., October 18, 1883.
Rowland, Dunbar, Encyclopedia of Mississippi History, Biographical. Southern Historical Association, 1916. Vol. I. pp. 787-89.
Young, Haran R., "Samuel J. Gholson", Subject File, Mississippi Department of Archives and History, Jackson.

Govan, Daniel Chevilette
"Gen. D. C. Govan Passes Away at Age of 84 Years", The Commercial Appeal, Memphis, Monday Morning, March 13, 1911.
"Gen. D. C. Govan", The Confederate Veteran, Vol. XIX, p. 444.

Gregg, John
Sykes, E. L., "Burial of Gen. John Gregg in Mississippi", The Confederate Veteran, Nashville, Tn., October, 1914, Vol XXII. pp. 463-464.
"John Gregg, Brigadier General, C.S.A., The Confederate Veteran, Nashville, March 1914, p. 125.
"When General Gregg Was Killed", The Confederate Veteran, Nashville, January, 1920, p. 12.
Wilson, Clyde, "Gregg-Hamilton..Aberdeen's Most Interesting Home", The Aberdeen Examiner, Aberdeen, Miss., March 14, 1985.
Timberlake, W. L., "In the Siege of Richmond and After", The Confederate Veteran, Nashville, October, 1921. Vol. XXIX. pp. 412-413.
Hamilton, Mrs. Charles Granville, "Gregg, Mary Frances Garth", Mother Monroe, Mother Monroe Publishing Co., Hamilton, Ms. 1979, F395.

Green, Martin Edward
Cotton, Gordon A., " CSA Generals' Graves Remain Unmarked, Too", The Vicksburg Evening Post, Vicksburg, December 3, 1978.
Werdemeyer, J. M., "Missourians East of the Mississippi", The Confederate Veteran, November, 1910, p. 502.
The Confederate Veteran, August, 1910, p. 361.
Diary of John A. Leavy, M.D., Vicksburg National Military Park, Vicksburg, Ms.
"Five Confederate generals died in Vicksburg's defense", Siege. The Vicksburg Evening Post, Summer, 1988.

Griffith, Richard

Davis, William C., Jefferson Davis: The Man and His Hour. A Biography, New York, Harper Collins, 1991, pp. 432-433.

Rainwater, P. L., "W.A. Montgomery's Record of the Raymond Fencibles", The Journal of Mississippi History,

"Gen. Griffith", The Daily Clarion, July 7, 1862.

" Griffith, Richard", Biographical and Historical Memoirs of Mississippi, The Goodspeed Publishing Company: Chicago, 1981. p. 826.

Magee, Rex B., "Only One Woman Heads Civil War Round Table-Jackson's", The Jackson Daily News, February 21, 1960.

"Civil War General Once Owned Property", The Jackson Daily News, August 11, 1968, p. 3.

Smith, Gustavus, "The Battle of Seven Pines, New York, 1891.

Sykes, E. T., "Walthall's Brigade", Mississippi History Society Publications, Vol. I. "Centenary Series" N. P. , 1916.

"The Late Col. William M. Inge", The Confederate Veteran, Nashville, January, 1901, Vol. IX, p. 20.

Sears, Stephen W., To The Gates of Richmond - The Peninsula Campaign, New York, Tickner & Fields, 1992, p. 266.

Dowdey, Clifford, The Seven Days, Boston, Little Brown & Co. 1964.

Interview with Ms. Genevieve Wilde Barksdale, great grandaughter of General Griffith, Ocean Springs, Mississippi, February, 1994.

Hogg, Joseph Lewis

Blakey, P. A., "Errors Corrected Concerning Gen. Hogg", The Confederate Veteran, Nashville, November, 1906, p.494.

Inge, Mrs. F. A., "Corinth, Miss., In Early War Days", The Confederate Veteran, Nashville, September, 1909, p. 442-444.

Blakey, P. A. "Brig. Gen. Joseph L. Hogg", The Confederate Veteran, Nashville, August 1907, Vol XV, p 379.

Humphreys, Benjamin Grubb

"The Funeral of Ex-Governor Humphreys", The Southern Reveille, Port Gibson, Claiborne County, Miss., December 30, 1882.

"Rev. D. A. Plauck on the Life and Character of the late Ex-Gov. Humphreys at his Funeral on the 27th of December, 1862", The Souther Reveille, Port Gibson, Claiborne County, Miss., January 27, 1883.

"Gen. B. G. Humphreys..A Greeting From the Grave", The Natchez Weekly Democrat, October 17, 1883.

"Humphreys Elected Under Johnson's Reconstruction", The Clarion Ledger, January 16, 1940.

"How Humphreys and Family Were Expelled From the Mansion by Military

Orders", The Clarion Ledger, April 16, 1908.

"One of Our First Ladies Back in Governor's Mansion", The Clarion Ledger-Jackson Daily News, October 28, 1955.

"When Governor Humphreys was Ejected From Office", The Clarion Ledger, May 3, 1899.

Magee, Rex B., "Mississippian Fired From West Point Was War Hero Under Lee", The Clarion Ledger, Jackson, Ms., March 15, 1952.

Lee, Stephen Dill

Bass, Frank, "S. D. Lee: A Man Of Vision, Whose Dreams Became Reality", The Commercial Dispatch, Columbus, Mississippi, August 4, 1985.

"Sketch of Gen. Lee by Chaplain J. W. Jones", The Vicksburg Post, Friday, May 28, 1908.

Ethridge, Tom, "Stephen D. Lee Set a High Standard of Heroic Service",

"Universal Grief-Vicksburgers Occupy Places of Honor", The Vicksburg Post, Monday, June 1, 1908.

"Brief Biography of Gen. Stephen D. Lee", The Vicksburg Evening Post, Thursday, May 28, 1908.

"Commnader Fights His Last Battle", The Daily State, Baton Rouge, La. May 28, 1908.

"Lieut. Gen. Stephen D. Lee Speaks", The Daily Herald, Vicksburg, Ms., October 8, 1899.

"Gallant Confederate Chieftain Obeys Summons of Supreme Commander", The Columbus Dispatch, Friday, May 29, 1908.

McIntire, Carl, "Stephen Lee Made Name in Military, Education", The Clarion Ledger, Jackson, Ms. February 15, 1987.

Saggus, James, "Stephen D. Lee: A Rare War Hero", The Clarion Ledger, January 6, 1966.

"Funeral Address- General Stephen D. Lee", The Baptist Record, July, 1908.

Lowrey, Mark Perrin

"Rand, Clayton, "Men Who Made the South", The Commercial Appeal, November 29, 1942.

"Death of Gen. Lowrey", The Southern Sentinel, Ripley, Ms. May 5, 1885.

The Baptist Record, Thursday, March 26, 1885.

Sumrall, Robbie Neal, A Light on the Hill- A History of Blue Mountain College, Nasville, Tn. Benson Printing Co., 1947, pp. 6-17.

Shearer, P. W., "Gen. Mark Perrin Lowrey",

General M. P. Lowrey, An Autobiograpy , Ripley, Mississippi, September 39, 1867, published in the Kennesaw Gazette, November 15, 1888.

Unidentified Newpaper Clippings in Scrapbook located in May Gardner

Black Alumni Room, Blue Mountain College, Blue Mountain, Ms.

Articles from Robert Talley, located in scrapbook of Modena Lowrey Berry "Mother Berry", Blue Mountain College, Blue Mountain, Ms.

Brown, Andrew, History of Tippah County, Mississippi: The First Century, The Tippah County Historical and Genealogical Society, Inc., 1976, p. 264.

Shearer, P. W., The Confederate Veteran, Nashville, Vol.XV, p. 13.

Lowry, Robert

"Robt. Lowry, Statesman and Soldier, Answers the Call", The Daily Clarion-Ledger, Jackson, Ms., January 20, 1910, p.1.

"Ex-Governor of Mississippi Dead", The Brandon News, Brandon, Rankin County, Miss., January 20, 1910, p. 1.

Richardson, Sarah, "Famous Rebel Buried in County", The Pearl Press, Pearl, Miss., October 12, 1978.

"Pay Last Tribute to Memory of Gov. Lowry", The Daily Clarion Ledger, Jackson, Ms., January 22, 1910.

"Hour For the Funeral of Gov. Lowry Changed to Noon", The Daily Clarion Ledger, Jackson, Ms., January 21, 1910.

"Gen. Robert Lowry", The Confederate Veteran, Nashville, April, 1910, p. 182.

McNair, Evander

"A Noble Man With a Noble War Record", The Hattiesburg American, Hattiesburg, Ms., November 14, 1902.

The Magnolia Gazette, November 15, 1902.

"Funeral of Gen. McNair", The Magnolia Gazette, Wednesday, November 19, 1902.

Bunn, H. G. Colonel Fourth Arkansas Infantry, C.S.A., "Gen. Evandar McNair", The Confederate Veteran, Nashville, Tenn., Vol. XI., June, 1903.

Martin, William Thompson

Walworth, Douglas, "General W. T. Martin in Confederate Army", The Daily Democrat, Natchez, June 8, 1908.

"General Martin Called to Rest", The Natchez Democrat, March 17, 1910.

"Volley and Taps at Grave of Gen. Martin", The Natchez Democrat, March 18, 1910.

"Biographical Sketch of General William Thompson Martin of Natchez, Mississippi", Martin Subject File, Mississippi Department of Archives and History, Jackson.

Sears, Claudius Wistar

"Death of Gen. C. W. Sears, The Oxford Eagle, February 19, 1891.

Diary of General Sears contained in Sword Featherston File, Mississippi Department of Archives and History, Jackson.

Riess, Karlem, "Claudius Wistar Sears, Soldier and Educator", The Journal of Mississippi History, ? pp. 128-137.

Rea, R. N., " Gen. G. W. Sears- A Pathetic Incident", The Confederate Veteran, p 327.

Sharp, Jacob Hunter

"Gallant Soldier Summoned Above", The Columbus Dispatch, September 19, 1907.

"Mathews, Craig, "Brigadier General Jacob Hunter Sharp, C.S.A.", given by his grandaughter Mrs. Frank Owen of Columbus, Mississippi in August, 1951.

"Gen. Jacob H. Sharp", The Confederate Veteran, November, 1907, Vol. XV, p. 516.

Banks, R. W. "Famous Mississippians", From Jacob Hunter Sharp File, Columbus Public Library.

Leavell, George W., "Battle of Franklin Remembrances", The Confederate Veteran, Nashville, pp. 500-502.

Smith, James Argyle

"General Smith is Dead", The Daily Clarion, December 6, 1901.

Tucker, William Feimster

"Gen. W. F. Tucker, The Facts of his Murder", The Weekly Clarion, Jackson, Ms., Sept. 29, 1881.

"Eulogy on the Life and Character of Gen. Tucker By Hon. J. R. Mcintosh at a Bar Meeting Held in Respect to His Memory", The Weekly Clarion, September 29, 1881.

"Tucker Relief Fund", The Weekly Clarion, Jackson, Ms., October 27, 1881.

" W. F. Tucker Funeral Services", The Weekly Clarion, Jackson, Ms. September 22, 1881.

"The Assassination of Gen. Tucker", The Weekly Clarion, September 22, 1881.

Heiss, Mrs. John, "Tucker, William Feimster", History of Chickasaw County, Chickasaw County Historical and Geneological Society, 1985.

Biography of General William Feimster Tucker contained in W. F. Tucker Subject File, Mississippi Archives And History, Jackson.

"Chickasaw's Martial Hero", The Commercial Appeal, Memphis, Tn., April 7, 1929.

Henderson, Richey, "Biographical Sketch of William F. Tucker", Subject File, Mississippi Department of Archives and History, Jackson.

Van Dorn, Earl

Roth, David E., "The Mysteries of Spring Hill, Tennessee", The Blue and Gray, October-November, 1984.

McIntire, Carl, "Sons of South", The Clarion Ledger, August 31, 1975.

Andrews, A. P., "Van Dorn Foils Yank Drive; Assassin's Gun Drops Him", The State Times, September 25, 1960.

"Rebel General Van Dorn Carved Fame Early as Indian Fighter", The State Times, September 18, 1960.

"Monument will be Erected Over the Grave of a Soldier Who Fell by a Civilian's Bullet", The Memphis Morning News, Memphis, Tn., March 1, 1903.

Thompson, Ray, "The Sword of Gen. Van Dorn", The Daily Herald, November 29, 1961.

Letter to Mr. Arthur B. Cater from Admiral Husband E. Kimmel dated 18 January, 1967, Van Dorn Subject File, Mississippi Department of Archives and History, Jackson.

"Obituary of Mrs. Caroline Van Dorn, wife of General Earl Van Dorn", Holly Spring South, Holly Springs, Ms., March 16, 1876.

Rowland, Dunbar, Encyclopedia of Mississippi History, Vol. II, pp. 847-849.

"The Killing of Van Dorn by Dr. Peters", The New York Times, May 19, 1863.

Golden, Wilson, "Van Dorn's Raid Recaptured", The Marshall Messenger, Holly Springs, Ms. April 8, 1981.

Walthall, Edward Carey

"Memorial Addresses of the Life and Character of Edward C. Walthall", May 26, 1898 - Feb 25, 1899, United States Senate.

Rand, Clayton, "Men Who Made the South", The Commercial Appeal, September 8, 1942.

McLemore, Richard Aubrey, A History of Mississippi- Volume Two, University and College Press of Mississippi, Hattiesburg, 1973, pp. 22-23.

"Edward Cary Walthall" The Yazoo Herald, Yazoo City, Ms., May 20, 1898.

"Hood's Tennessee Campaign", The Confederate Veteran, Vol. XV, Sept. 1907, p. 401-409.

"Death of Sen. Walthall", The Holly Springs Reporter, Holly Springs, Ms., April 28, 1898.

Papers and Unidentified Newspaper articles in Walthall Subject File, Mississippi Department of Archives and History, Jackson.

York, Zebulon

"General Zebulon York", The Natchez Weekly Democrat, Natchez, Ms., August 8, 1900.

PUBLICATIONS

Faust, Patricia, *Historical Times Illustrated Encylopedia of the Civil War,* Harper & Row, New York, 1986.

Rowland, Dunbar, *Encyclopedia of Mississippi History, Biographical,* Southern Historical Association, 1916., vol I, II, III.

Godspeeds, *Memoirs of Mississippi*

Warner, Ezra, *Generals in Gray*, Louisiana State University Press, Baton Rouge, London, 1959.

Miller, Trevelyan, *The Photographic History of the Civil War,* "The Armies and the Leaders", Castle Books, New York, 1911.

Welsh, Jack D., *Medical Histories of the Confederate Generals,* (In Press), Kent State University Press, Kent, Ohio.

IN SEARCH OF CONFEDERATE ANCESTORS: THE GUIDE, *by J.H. Segars, edited by John McGlone; Southern Heritage Press, P.O. Box 1615, Murfreesboro, TN 37133-1615; ISBN 0-9631963-4-0; $10, paper; 112pp.*

This is Volume IX of the Journal of Confederate History Series. It should become a classic, the standard by which such references are judged. From its prologue ("Why Search for Confederate Ancestors?") to its index, the book is filled with information on sources, where to find them, and how to use them. Easily followed instructions provide "how to" for the research. Addresses and phone numbers are listed for state archives and libraries, along with listings of the types of data available in each. Alternative sources, such as the Confederate Research Center at Hillsboro, are also given. We recommend that each camp of the Sons of Confederate Veterans have at least one copy of The Guide, to assist potential members in locating and documenting their required ancestry. If you use this book and can't find a Confederate ancestor, "Friend, you ain't got one!"

Ralph Green
Past Commander-in-Chief
Sons of the Confederate Veterans

Photo Credits

Pages 7, 31, 115, 153, 181
Collection of the State of Mississippi Historical Museum

Pages 11, 20, 36, 43, 49, 53, 74, 89, 95, 103
Mississippi Department of Archives and History

Pages 17, 24, 69, 123, 129, 135, 141, 145, 148, 161
Library of Congress

Pages 61, 79, 83, 165
U. S. Army Military History Institute, Carlisle, Pa.

Pages 109, 119
Millers Pictorial History of the Civil War, 1911.

Page 175
The Confederate Veteran

Pages 2, 3 ,6, 10, 16, 19, 23, 27, 28, 30, 35, 40, 42, 48, 52, 57, 60, 65, 66, 68, 73, 78, 82, 85, 86, 88, 92, 94, 100, 102, 106, 108, 112, 114, 118, 122, 126, 128, 132, 134, 138, 140, 144, 147, 150, 152, 158, 160, 164, 172, 174, 178, 180, 185.
Harold A. Cross

DORO PLANTATION
Received as a fee in a famous Indian lawsuit in the 1840's by Charles Clark, later Civil War governor, 1863-65. He is buried on the grounds of this plantation.
MISSISSIPPI DEPARTMENT OF ARCHIVES AND HISTORY

OCTAVIA DOCKERY
1865
APRIL 22. 1949
MISTRESS
OF
GOAT CASTLE
BRIG GEN
THOMAS P DOCKERY
RESERVE
CORPS OF ARK
CSA
DEC 18 1833
FEB 26 1898

CONFEDERATE DEAD